THE UNEXPECTED ADVENTURES OF
MARTIN
FREEMAN

D053158B

THE UNEXPECTED ADVENTURES OF
MARTIN FREEMAN

Neil Daniels

JOHN BLAKE

Published by John Blake Publishing Ltd,
3 Bramber Court, 2 Bramber Road,
London W14 9PB, England

www.johnblakepublishing.co.uk

www.facebook.com/johnblakebooks
twitter.com/jblakebooks

This edition published in 2015

ISBN: 978 1 78418 337 0

British Library Cataloguing-in-Publication Data:

A catalogue record for this book is available from the British Library.

Design by www.envydesign.co.uk

Printed in Great Britain by CPI Group (UK) Ltd

1 3 5 7 9 10 8 6 4 2

Papers used by John Blake Publishing are natural, recyclable products made from
wood grown in sustainable forests. The manufacturing processes conform to the
environmental regulations of the country of origin.

Every attempt has been made to contact the relevant copyright-holders, but some
were unobtainable. We would be grateful if the appropriate people could contact us.

ABOUT THE AUTHOR

Neil Daniels is the author of *Matthew McConaughey – The Biography* (John Blake) and over a dozen books on music. His titles include *AC/DC – The Early Years & Bon Scott*; *Metallica: The Early Years And The Rise Of Metal*; *Iron Maiden: The Ultimate Unauthorized History Of The Beast*; *Beer Drinkers and Hell Raisers: A ZZ Top Guide*; *High Stakes & Dangerous Men – The UFO Story*; *Bon Jovi Encyclopaedia*; *Don't Stop Believin': The Untold Story of Journey*; and *Reinventing Metal: The True Story Of Pantera and the Tragically Short Life of Dimebag Darrell*. He has written for a number of publications including *The Guardian*, *Rock Sound* and *Record Collector*.

Neil lives in the north-west of England.

His official website is www.neildanielsbooks.com

CONTENTS

CHAPTER ONE

EARLY LIFE AND BECOMING AN ACTOR

'My journey is to try to be good in interesting things. This is the thing:
I don't, necessarily, want to do all films, like films are the validation
of why I wanted to be an actor, you know.'
FREEMAN SPEAKING TO *EMPIRE* MAGAZINE, 2005

As one of the most revered and popular actors in Great
Britain, Martin Freeman is not only a household name
but a national treasure.

An actor in the grand tradition of such contemporary
theatrical greats as Patrick Stewart and Ian McKellen, Martin
Freeman can exercise his obvious thespian talents in theatre
just as well as in TV or film and even the radio. He is a character
actor who can in one year appear in a comedy film, only to
then star in an epic fantasy-film series and a darkly twisted
American drama. He is Dr John Watson, Lester Nygaard, Bilbo
Baggins and Arthur Dent. Much like the late Alec Guinness,
Martin Freeman is a chameleon who can hop from one role to
the next with considerable aplomb.

As is the case with just about anyone in the arts-and-entertainment industry, Freeman was a jobbing actor before he found his footing and made a name for himself in such notable shows as *Sherlock* and *Fargo*. But what prompted him to become an actor? What drives him to commit to such a varied range of roles? Who is Martin Freeman?

Martin John Christopher Freeman was born on 8 September 1971 in Aldershot, Hampshire. He was the youngest of five children. His parents, Philomena (née Norris) and Geoffrey Freeman, a naval officer, separated when Freeman was a child.

'It didn't seem strange at the time but I suppose it is,' Freeman admitted to the *London Evening Standard*'s Bruce Dessau in 2005 concerning his parents' separation. 'It was just the way things were. It was quite a civilised separation and when my mum was back on her feet financially, I moved back with her.'

Freeman was a creative and imaginative child and those talents would later manifest themselves in his lengthy body of work as an actor.

'Dreams can be extremely vivid, so that's why they're so troubling to us some of the time and why they're so real,' Freeman explained to the *NYC Movie Guru* in 2007. 'When I was six years old, I woke up and my family had just bought a donkey and we kept it in the kitchen – then I woke up [for real] and went downstairs and I was like, "Where's the donkey?" I think it's the Australian Aborigines who considered dreamed time to be actually more pertinent to life than waking life because it can tell you so much about your life and what your fears and hopes are.'

After the divorce Freeman lived with his dad but, sadly, when

Martin was just ten years old, his father died of a heart attack. The family then moved to the outskirts of South London and Freeman settled back in with his mother and stepfather James, who ran pubs.

When Martin Freeman appeared in a 2009 episode of the popular BBC genealogy series *Who Do You Think You Are?* he learned that his grandfather, Leonard Freeman, was a medic during World War II. Leonard was part of an ill-fated British Expeditionary Force that journeyed to France. Medical records state that he was killed two days before the evacuation from Dunkirk began in 1940. Leonard was an officer in the 150th Field Ambulance unit and his war diary can be found in the Imperial War Museum.

Leonard's father, Freeman's great-grandfather, Richard, was born blind in 1853 and had been a piano tuner and organist at St Andrew's Church in West Tarring. He was educated at a special school in Hampstead, which is now run by the Royal London Society for the Blind and is based in Kent. Its extensive records show that Richard lived an independent life and was trained as a musician. He became a music teacher in Kingston upon Hull.

Freeman learned more about his great-grandfather. Richard lived a comfortable but simple life and joined the English middle classes. He was married with a family and lived in a large house in West Tarring. He became an organist at St Andrew's Church in his hometown. His first wife, Fanny, died in 1891 but he later remarried, to a woman named Emily. No death certificate exists for Fanny.

An 1894 entry in the parish magazine reads, 'The

circumstances under which the post of organist at Tarring became vacant are well known to our readers.'

Freeman was not able to gain any information about what appears to have been a scandal, which was presumably to do with the remarriage. After the death of his second wife, Richard moved to the north of England and started a new life for himself. Living in Hull, he became a music teacher and married his third wife, Aida – Leonard's mother and Freeman's great-grandmother. Freeman discovered that one of Aida's grandchildren was born blind and that the couple lost six children.

Martin learned upon a visit to Great Ormond Street Hospital and from the Royal Society of Medicine that Aida more than likely suffered from syphilis. He came to this conclusion based upon two facts: her brother died of the disease and there is a glaring similarity to the way her children died, which suggests that she more than likely caught the disease a second time from her husband, Richard. Aida, however, raised a large family and lived into her nineties, remarrying twice.

'You kind of wonder how many extraordinary characters everyone has got in their family,' said Freeman in the programme, 'that we're all made up of these extraordinary people.'

As a child, family history did not seem all that important to Freeman, as it generally doesn't to many children, but Martin has since then become fixated by his family's past.

'I used to watch *Sleuth* with Michael Caine and Laurence Olivier every day as a kid,' Freeman said to the *Daily Express*'s Cheryl Stonehouse. 'I was eleven and loved it. I thought, "I could do this acting lark".'

This 1972 critically revered film directed by Joseph L.

Mankiewicz is about a wealthy man who loves games and the theatre and sets up a battle of wits for his wife's lover, whom he invites to meet him at his house. It was the sort of intelligent, well-crafted and marvellously acted drama that Freeman would hope to star in one day.

Freeman was also a big fan of comedy – notably *The Goodies*, Laurel and Hardy and *Tom and Jerry*. He also enjoyed the slapstick comedy of the American star Jerry Lewis. He would watch the routines and sketches and make mental notes about timing and facial expressions and see how the actors reacted to each other. It was all subconscious preparation for his later vocation.

Martin's family were not overtly religious, though he was raised a Roman Catholic. Martin has, since childhood, struggled with religion; though his faith in Catholicism has remained intact. Before enrolling at Brooklands College, where he studied media, Martin was a student at Salesian School, a Roman Catholic comprehensive in Chertsey.

When quizzed on the subject by a journalist for *The Scotsman* in 2009, he responded, 'When people have a go at organised religion, it's not necessarily people who have been reading Chomsky and come to this great idea by a lot of research. A lot of it is laziness. Organised religion, organised anything, requires commitment and requires an engagement with something. A lot of the time, we don't want to commit. Of course, if you talk about the Spanish Inquisition, that's the bad end of organised religion. But organised means there's more than ten people involved, because it was an idea people liked. I don't see how you get round it.'

From a young age, it appears that Freeman dreamed of the

Big Smoke and finding fame and fortune in the city. Life in the English suburbs could be stifling; London would be a great source of inspiration and pride for him.

Freeman discussed his earliest memories of growing up in London with the *London Evening Standard*'s Hannah Nathanson: 'I grew up in the suburbs so I remember arriving at Waterloo and seeing Big Ben and the coloured lights on top of the Southbank Centre and thinking, "Wow!" I also remember walking along the south side of the Thames by HMS *Belfast* with my mum and it was just a wasteland. It's amazing what's been done to that area now.'

Martin was an asthmatic child, prone to fainting and hip pain and, as a consequence of his ailment, he had to undergo an operation on his leg. He had what is medically known as Perthes disease, which made his hip bone soften and gave him a slight limp when he walked. He did not want people to feel sorry for him and it didn't stop him from playing for the British National Squash Squad between the ages of nine and fourteen. His love for squash, however, was overshadowed when he discovered acting.

'There was very little drama and performance at my school,' he admitted to *The Scotsman* in 2009, 'so I've never forgotten the people who did encourage me and I've thought whether it would be a good idea to even get in touch with them and just say thanks, because they really opened a door for me mentally and emotionally – that's really important.'

Freeman has since admitted he didn't have the discipline to proceed with squash and neither did he enjoy the idea that something he did for pleasure could potentially become a job.

How ironic, given his future career.

He admitted to being something of a show-off at school; there was an extrovert inside him bubbling to jump out. His peers found him quite funny and they would say things like, 'You should have your own TV show.' Freeman, as with many actors, has a two-sided personality – there's the coy, quiet persona but also the funny, more extrovert side to him that likes to show off.

There is also an artistic streak in his family: his elder brother Tim was in the 1980s Brighton-based pop group Frazier Chorus, who released two albums on Virgin Records – *Sue* in 1989 and *Ray* in 1991. A third and final album, *Wide Awake*, was released in 1995. Jamie Freeman later became a musician and website designer and their cousin Ben Norris became a stand-up comedian. However, none of them reached the heights of fame and success that Martin attained in later life. 'I don't think it was a surprise that I ended up as an actor, and it was anything but a disappointment,' Martin told Miranda Sawyer of *The Guardian* in 2005. 'My parents gave me the knowledge that reading isn't a bad thing, and admitting to liking a painting doesn't make you an arse-bandit. And that wouldn't have been a problem either.'

His family, including his mother and late father, encouraged artistic freedom and expression from an early age, which no doubt influenced Martin's decision to pursue a career as an actor.

'I think I was influenced by the fact there was the environment at home that, we're creating things, and expressing yourself artistically wasn't to be frowned upon, so in that, I was always aware that it was OK to write or read,' Freeman later explained to *Dark Horizon*'s Paul Fischer. 'You didn't have to pretend to be stupid or pretend that you weren't interested in things that you were interested in, so there was always the environment where it was open for that to happen. I guess probably seeing films at a very early age, because we all watched telly, was a strong influence.'

Freeman embraced music and film but, in terms of literature, he dipped in and out of books. Literature is often the perfect form of escapism for children who want to expand their imagination and there was one book that made an impact with some of his generation: Douglas Adams's *The Hitchhiker's Guide to the Galaxy*. It is a story that would have much more of an impact on Freeman's life as an adult than it did as a child.

'I was at an age when it either kind of hooked you in or it didn't, and it didn't,' he admitted to Alona Wartofsky of *The Washington Post*. 'That wasn't really where I was at when I was thirteen.'

So what did he read when growing up?

'George Orwell, I suppose... *Animal Farm*, *Homage to Catalonia*. I liked all his stuff,' he explained to Wartofsky. 'I read *Animal Farm* when I was eleven, and it remained my favourite book, really.'

Aged fifteen, Freeman joined the Teddington Youth Theatre, which would be a major catalyst for his ambition to become an actor; it was at this point in his life when he found his calling, as it were.

'It was an outlet for my showing off,' he admitted to Andrew Duncan of *Reader's Digest*. 'Also, I thought I could bring down the Thatcher government with the power of my acting. And

I did. A mere five years later she went. You tell me that was coincidence. I think I hoped actors could have some influence.'

But it wasn't just about showing off. As with any artistic endeavour, acting gave Freeman an outlet to express the emotional turmoil that was bubbling inside him. There is a pent-up energy and frustration within him. Freeman told *The Guardian*'s Miranda Sawyer in 2005: 'I'm not a practising Catholic or I wouldn't be living unwed with a woman, and I don't think all poofs are going to hell, and I don't think everyone who's had an abortion is damned, most of my friends are atheists and I understand atheism, I get it, but I happen to be a theist. I believe in our answerableness to something else. You're not the only cunt in the world.'

He told Rebecca Hardy of the *Mail Online* in 2009: 'My first moral touchstone was Jesus. So how about that for an uphill struggle? Jesus, Gandhi and Martin Luther King – anything less than that and you're failing. It's ridiculous, but I also know it's true of myself.'

Sherlock co-creator Mark Gatiss would reiterate this point to *Entertainment Weekly*'s Josh Rottenberg in 2014: 'He's got such funny bones and he's a very angry man as well, which provides a great deal of laughs. The thing we always have to do with Martin is take lines out [of the script] because he says, "Well, I can just do that with a look." And he's always right.'

It was not until he turned seventeen that he had enough confidence to pursue acting on a professional level. He enrolled at the famed Central School of Speech and Drama in London and immersed himself in theatre productions of *As You Like It*, *Much Ado About Nothing* and *Romeo and Juliet*.

He soon began appearing in TV shows and theatre productions, as well as some notable radio broadcasts, all of which gave him invaluable experience and, perhaps more importantly, contacts in the industry. Naturally, he was up against fierce competition, as there is in any creative field, yet Freeman, while neither arrogant nor rude, was rather determined and confident of what he could and could not do.

'Michael Caine, Tom Courtenay and Al Pacino made me want to act,' Freeman said to Hannah Nathanson of the *London Evening Standard*. 'I've always been interested in men with a vulnerable side.' Michael Caine and Tom Courtenay, both of whom have been knighted by Her Majesty Queen Elizabeth II, are two of Britain's most respected actors of the stage and screen, while Al Pacino is one of America's great cinema thespians: an icon of contemporary American cinema.

Freeman is, perhaps, more in line with Caine: an actor who can handle comedy and drama and who can move between genres and stays, for the most part, steadfastly English or, rather, 'London'. Freeman would soon learn, as Caine did, that acting is more than a full-time vocation and that, in order to pay the bills and earn a living, sacrifices have to be made. Caine once said that there are two films you do as an actor – films for the money (*The Muppet Christmas Carol* and *Jaws 4: The Revenge*) and films for critical respect as an actor (*Little Voice* and *Harry Brown*). This was certainly a path Freeman was going to follow. Doesn't every actor? Every thespian has to make a buck somehow. An actor could be in work one year and out of work the next.

Michael Caine was born in Rotherhithe, east London on 14 March 1933 and made his breakthrough roles in the 1960s with such films as *Zulu* (1964), *The Ipcress File* (1965), *Alfie* – which gained him an Oscar nomination – (1966), *The Italian Job* (1969) and *Battle of Britain* (1969). His 1970s roles include *Get Carter* (1971), *The Last Valley* (1971), *Sleuth* (1972), for which he earned his second Oscar nomination, *The Man Who Would Be King* (1975) and *A Bridge Too Far* (1978). Many of these films would influence the young Martin Freeman. Since the 1970s, Caine has starred in comedies, dramas, thrillers and action films, as well as science-fiction movies such as *Children of Men* and *Inception*. He is known for his distinctive cockney accent, which he has rarely hidden. Indeed, much like fellow Londoner Bob Hoskins, Caine has used his cockney accent to his advantage. There's no question that Caine's eclectic choice of roles continues to have a profound effect on Freeman, and his influence on him goes back to the age of eleven, when Martin watched the film *Sleuth*.

Tom Courtenay, on the other hand, is best known for his work in TV and theatre, although his cinematic career had its heyday in the 1960s with such stellar films as *The Loneliness of the Long Distance Runner* (1962), *Billy Liar* (1963) and *Doctor Zhivago* (1965).

There was a humorous side to Freeman which came to the fore amongst his friends, though in larger social circles he could be rather coy – it is not uncommon for an actor to be shy offstage or behind the camera. There is a perception that Freeman always wanted to be a comedian because of some of the roles he chose later in life, but that was never the case.

'When I was at youth theatre and drama school, I never thought people would mistake me for a stand-up,' he admitted to *Digital Spy*'s Morgan Jeffery in 2011. 'A lot of people still think I'm a stand-up or that I have [a comedy] background. That was never the plan at all. I like being funny – I like making people laugh and I like people making me laugh – but that was never the reason I wanted to get into acting. [Although] it's part of it, because all of my favourite films and plays have both [comedy and drama] in.'

Another passion of Freeman's besides acting has always been music. He'd been buying records since he was nine or ten years old and, when CDs arrived during his teens, he spent all his money buying the latest music on discs. He would one day acquire an expensive collection of thousands of CDs and vinyl records. Freeman's love is of American rhythm and blues, and soul.

'When I was much younger, I would've looked at a record and thought, "That guy on the cover has a great afro. This is probably fucking amazing,"' he said to *Tiny Mix Tapes* in 2007 about his record-buying habits.

Freeman described having a 'Catholic taste in music', which he elaborated on during the same interview: 'Catholic in the literal sense, meaning broad or universal. You don't want to say you like everything, because that means you like a lot of shit. But as far as genres are concerned, I don't want to limit myself. I don't want to be one of those people who say, "I don't like any fucking folk records."'

Freeman was also a minor political activist in his youth, which perhaps stemmed from his Catholic upbringing. He was anti-Thatcher. The now deceased British prime minister – the UK's first and, thus far, only female PM – was notorious among the working classes and those with left-wing views. She was something of a tyrannical figure in the north of England, especially.

He explained his politics to *Reader's Digest*'s Andrew Duncan: 'I sold *Militant* [a Socialist Party newspaper] on the street. My politics have dissipated into anger – not about anything specific, but a lot of things, a lot of people. Anger is a useful tool. I don't mean smashing people over the head, but our British cynicism keeps a check on bullshit. It's not a bad thing to have a social conscience, although I've never wanted to go into politics. I'd be scared. You name it, I'd ban it.'

It's lucky for us, then, that Freeman saw his future in acting and decided to pursue his ambition with discipline and zest.

CHAPTER TWO

GETTING A BREAK ON THE SMALL SCREEN

'I'm a well-behaved actor and a well-choosing actor because if I choose to do something, then you better believe that I'm committed to it. If I didn't like something and thought it needed change, I either wouldn't do it or would want a script doctor's fee.'
Freeman speaking to *NYC Movie Guru*, 2007

Working on TV shows and on independent films is often the best way to gain experience. Freeman was inspired by the directors and producers of the late 1960s and 1970s in an era of 'New Hollywood' after the demise of the studio system, when studios had actors and directors under contract and could dictate which films they could and could not make. The studio system was almost Orwellian in its dictatorship.

With the studio system broken and the ground-breaking 'French New Wave' still in mind, which brought unconventional forms of storytelling to cinema by such film-making intellectuals and scholars as Jean Luc Godard and Francois Truffaut, a generation of American film students – baby boomers born in the 1940s and raised in the prosperous 1950s – out of either the suburbs of California and small-town America or, conversely, from the tough streets of New York, broke new ground with often violent and unconventional films, such as *Bonnie and Clyde* and *Easy Rider* and, in the 1970s, the first two *Godfather* films and *Taxi Driver*. Directors like Francis Ford Coppola, Brian De Palma and Martin Scorsese worked on low-budget exploitation B-movies for Roger Corman, which gave them the experience and knowledge they needed to make their own films. They were not only film students who studied the history and theory of cinema but they were also film fanatics who were as familiar with European cinema as with what dominated the US market.

However, while such controversial auteurs as Scorsese and De Palma refused to be censored and conform to box-office needs, George Lucas and Steven Spielberg arrived in Hollywood motivated by a different school of thought, with influences that ranged from comic books to sci-fi movies and the suburban American culture of their youth, as shown in Lucas's classic *American Graffiti*. Before Lucas hit gold with *Star Wars* in 1977, his first movie was an interesting low-budget, dystopian science-fiction tale called *THX-1138* but it didn't attract the kind of audience that *Star Wars* did. These blockbuster Hollywood films, however, were not to Freeman's taste. He aligns himself more with such masterful film-makers as Coppola and Scorsese and two of their most prominent actors, Robert DeNiro and Al Pacino. *The Godfather*, *Dog Day Afternoon*, *Taxi Driver* and *Scarface*: these are Freeman's inspirations as far as American cinema goes. They are jaw-droppingly outstanding films with the highest quality of directing, acting and writing. They inspired Freeman to act and they continue to inspire him to this day, as he told Jamie

Watt of *Ask Men* in 2012: 'I wanted to be an actor because I saw *Dog Day Afternoon*, you know what I mean?'

Al Pacino is one of Freeman's acting heroes. A method actor taught by the famed thespian teacher Lee Strasberg, Pacino is a bona fide American icon. Known for playing Italian-American gangsters and mobsters, such as Michael Corleone in *The Godfather* and Tony Montana in *Scarface*, he has also appeared in a number of roles as tough-talking streetwise New York Cops, police officers and lawyers. Some of his iconic roles include *Dog Day Afternoon* (one of Freeman's favourite movies), *Carlito's Way*, *Glengarry Glen Ross*, *Serpico*, ...*And Justice for All* and *The Panic in Needle Park*. Although Pacino isn't known for his theatrical work, he is an avid fan of Shakespeare and made his directorial debut with the excellent documentary *Looking for Richard*, about Richard III, which Freeman has no doubt seen. Pacino finally won a much-deserved Oscar for his performance as Frank Slade in *Scent of a Woman* in 1992.

Robert DeNiro, Freeman's other American acting icon, was turned down for the role of Michael Corleone in *The Godfather* but was cast as the young Vito Carleone in the stunning sequel, *The Godfather Part II*. Freeman is a huge admirer of these films. DeNiro made a name for himself after his collaborations with New York director Martin Scorsese in such films as *Mean Streets*, *Taxi Driver* and *Raging Bull* and, later, *Goodfellas* and *Casino*. Some of his other best-known performances include roles in *The Deer Hunter*, *Awakenings*, *Midnight Run* and *A Bronx Tale*, the latter of which he also directed. DeNiro has also ventured into comedy of late, with films like *Analyze This* and *Meet The Parents*. DeNiro and Pacino teamed up for the highly revered police procedural flick *Heat* and later reunited in *Righteous Kill*, an average cop movie at best which received mixed reviews, as most critics cited disappointment that the two screen legends would appear in a fairly average cop flick after the incredible reception *Heat* received.

Freeman has spent much of his adult life studying his favourite actors and films and learning from them as he refines his thespian skills, frequently quoting the likes of Al Pacino in interviews to the press. 'How I became famous was from *The Office*, so that's sort of what people associate me with,' he said to journalists at a press junket for Warner's in 2013. 'I am not putting myself in the same category as Al Pacino, but Al Pacino's first scene was Michael Corleone and that casts a long shadow, if that makes sense?'

By 1997 Freeman was confident enough to begin taking on roles and attending auditions. He wasn't successful at every audition but that's nothing out of the ordinary in such a competitive industry, even for well-known actors.

He made his first appearance on TV at the age of twenty-six in an episode of the long-running British-TV police series *The Bill*, which aired on 9 January 1997 and was the third episode of series thirteen. As one of the most remembered British TV shows of all time, *The Bill* ran from 1984 to 2010 and chronicled the work of London Met Officers at the fictional Sun Hill police station. Though Freeman had only a minor appearance as the character Craig Parnell in an episode titled 'Mantrap', it was his first professional role in front of the camera and a good stepping stone to more work.

Freeman then had a cameo role as the character Stuart in an episode of the acclaimed BBC drama *This Life*, which aired on 17 March 1997. In the episode, entitled 'Last Tango in Southwark', Freeman is seen stealing money from the bedroom of Milly and Egg (these are two of the main characters) after a house party. Martin then unknowingly drinks Egg's urine from a can, thinking it is beer. As with *The Bill*, *This Life* was one of the most popular TV series of the 1990s. Though it only ran for two series, it was highly revered and considered part of the 'Britpop' and 'Cool Britannia' era of the 1990s.

The roles were slowly coming in for Freeman as he was making contacts and attending auditions, like any other jobbing actor hoping to find that one big break to launch his career.

He was next cast in the music video for the Faith No More song 'I Started A Joke', a cover of the Bee Gees' 1968 song. Faith No More's version, though recorded in 1995, was released in 1998, after the group disbanded. It features on their greatest-hits album *Who Cares A Lot?*. Directed by Vito Rocco, the video also features Shaun Dingwall, performance artist David Hoyle as the karaoke singer, and Michelle Butterly of the ITV series *Benidorm*. It was filmed on 8 September 1998.

Following his appearances in *The Bill* and *This Life*, Freeman was cast as Ricky Beck in a 1998 episode of British TV hospital drama *Casualty* called 'She Loved The Rain', which was broadcast on 17 October. *Casualty* is one of Britain's longest running TV dramas and was first broadcast on 6 September 1986. The series focuses on Holby City Hospital in Wyvern, a fictional county in south-west England.

Titanic star Kate Winslet spoke about her 1993 appearance in *Casualty* to the *Radio Times*: 'In England, it almost seems to be part of a jobbing actor's training [to appear in *Casualty*]. As far as I was concerned it was a great episode, a great part. Appearing in *Casualty* taught me a big lesson in how to be natural in front of the camera.'

Interestingly, a survey was carried out by the *Radio Times* in March 2004, which concluded that *Casualty* has cast more future stars than any other British television series. The list is rather impressive, as it reads like a 'who's who' of contemporary British actors of stage and screen. Besides Kate Winslet, other notable actors to have appeared on the series include Orlando Bloom, Minnie Driver, Christopher Eccleston, Tom Hiddleston, Parminder Nagra, Sadie Frost, Ray Winstone, David Walliams, Jonny Lee Miller, Helen Baxendale, Robson Green, Brenda Fricker and, of course, Martin Freeman. *Casualty* has also featured such established actors as Norman Wisdom, Amanda Redman, Anita Dobson, Jenny Seagrove, Rula Lenska, Prunella Scales, Celia Imrie, Toyah Willcox, Maureen Lipman, Frances Barber, Andrew Sachs, Russ Abbot, Stephanie Beacham and Michelle Collins in small roles or cameos.

Freeman next cropped up as the character Brendan in an episode of the first series of *Picking Up The Pieces*, about a team of paramedics involved in life-or-death events, which aired on 10 December 1998. He also appeared as Frank in a 1998 short film called *I Just Want to Kiss You*, written and directed by Jamie Thraves, best known for his work on music videos for Radiohead, Coldplay and Blur.

Christopher Campbell of *Film School Rejects* wrote, '… this French New Wave-style throwback has Freeman looking very young and very skinny and actually quite goofy as a guy just hanging out with his mate and meeting girls and getting into trouble with his dad. The goofiness is a bit surprising if you primarily think of Freeman as the straight man of *The Office* and *Hitchhiker's Guide* and other such gigs. I certainly don't know of him doing a lot of voices and vocal sound effects and the sort of spry physicality he exhibits in the short these days.'

The following year he cropped up as 'The Car Owner' in a TV special called *Exhaust*.

By the turn of the century Freeman began appearing in more high-profile TV series. Actors, as with any self-employed freelance person, do not turn down jobs, because they never know when they will be next employed. Indeed, any and all freelance jobs are a gamble.

'I wasn't raking it in but I was raking work in,' he admitted to *Dark Horizon*'s Paul Fischer. 'I always did work that I was happy with, not work that made me famous or work that made me rich, but work that made me very happy and it was always valid work, so the first five years didn't feel hard at all.'

In 2000 Freeman starred in a few notable TV series and he very slowly began to get noticed. He starred as various characters in the six episodes of *Bruiser*, a BBC2 comedy-sketch show that ran from 18 February to 12 March. Written by David Mitchell and Robert Webb of *Mitchell And Webb* fame, with additional writers Ricky Gervais and Richard Ayoade, *Bruiser* starred Olivia Colman, David Mitchell, Robert Webb, Martin Freeman, Matthew Holness and Charlotte Hudson.

The series showed early on just how terrific Freeman is as a character actor.

In one sketch he is a paranoid, fairly pathetic man who mulls over every situation in his life, constantly overanalysing things. He soon starts to think that that some situations he finds himself in make him look like a pervert, stalker or paedophile and he randomly shouts out to the astonishment of those around him that he isn't such a person at all. In another sketch he is disrupted by a puppet called Sparky (voiced by Webb) as he tries to entice the bank manager on a romantic date. Freeman featured in several more hilarious sketches, including one where he constantly calls out a builder for being overly touchy so the builder attacks him. Martin also crops up in a sketch as a man in a pub who tries to impress a woman by being silly but injures himself in the process. In another sketch he plays an archaeologist on a dig, but it becomes evident that his enthusiasm far outweighs his knowledge. He also plays a pimp who behaves frivolously whenever anything sexual is mentioned, and a man who pays for photos in a photo booth, only to realise after collecting them that a man had been standing behind him, pulling silly faces.

Freeman was next cast as Jaap, a Dutch drug taker and general idiot, in two episodes of *Lock, Stock*, which ran for just seven episodes in 2000 and was an offshoot TV series of the acclaimed 1998 British gangster film, *Lock, Stock and Two Smoking Barrels*. It was commissioned by Ginger Productions: the production company owned by TV presenter Chris Evans. The series was first shown on Channel 4 and starred Ralph Brown, Daniel Caltagirone, Del Synnott, Scott Maslen and

Shaun Parkes. The rhyming slang of the London East End did not make the series exactly viewer friendly and it sunk without a trace. These sort of gritty roles were a reflection of where Freeman endeavoured to go as an actor, which stemmed from his interest in Pacino and DeNiro films. 'I'm not particularly interested in playing the smoothie, unless something 'orrible happens or unless something really interesting happens to the smoothie,' he admitted to Simon Houpt of *The Globe And Mail*. 'You might as well just make infomercials, if you just want to be smooth, or suave. If you're in it just because you want to, you know, ride a Harley and play James Bond, you're basically a model. And that's valid, as well, that's fine – but life isn't about that.'

Freeman had also made a return to the theatre in the early 2000 production of *Jump Mr Malinoff, Jump* written by first-time dramatist Toby Whithouse. The play won the Verity Bargate Award, which was founded in memory of the Soho Theatre Company's founder where *Jump Mr Malinoff, Jump* was staged.

The *Daily Telegraph*'s Charles Spencer wrote of the play, 'Jonathan Lloyd's production marvellously captures the piece's strengths, finding both the laughs and the play's moving undertow of pain. And there's excellent work from Paul Chequer and Justin Salinger as the brothers, and from Laura Sadler and Martin Freeman as the brothers' disruptive friends. You leave convinced you have encountered a distinctive and hugely sympathetic new talent.'

Despite Freeman's interest in grittier roles and his love of Pacino and DeNiro, when he finally got his breakthrough role, it would be far removed from that genre.

CHAPTER THREE

MOVING INTO FILMS

'I guess pre-*The Office*, which was the thing that made me famous,
I was more of a blank canvas for people.'
FREEMAN SPEAKING TO OLIVER FRANKLIN IN *GQ*, 2013

Freeman was concerned that he would be typecast as an actor, so he tried his hand at various roles. He was cast as Solomon in the 2000 film *The Low Down* from the writer and director of the 1998 short film *I Just Want to Kiss You*, which also happened to star Freeman.

The Low Down was his debut role in a feature-length film. The film, released on 27 January 2001, is essentially a story about real-life relationships. BBC's Michael Thomson wrote, 'Director Jamie Thraves (who made the video for Radiohead's 'Just') knows how to create power from an accumulation of detail, wee asides, and glances but also forgets that daily drabness can be rather dull to watch. Neither are his hand-held camera or preference for short scenes always easy on the eye, but well-acted authenticity from the cast makes up for it.'

Freeman then had a cameo as 'the Doctor' in an episode of *Black Books* called 'Cooking The Books', which was broadcast on

29 September 2000. The episode sees bookshop owner Bernard Black struggle with the everyday tasks of running a shop. A hilarious BAFTA-winning comedy, *Black Books* was created by Dylan Moran (who stars in the lead role of bookshop owner Bernard Black) and Graham Linehan. It ran for three series and focuses on the London bookshop Black Books and follows Black and his assistant Manny Bianco, played by comedian Bill Bailey, and their friend Fran Katzenjammer, played by Tamsin Greig. The DVD audio commentary for *Shaun of the Dead* makes a reference to the series, saying that *Black Books* is thought of as a sister show to the cult 1999 Channel 4 series *Spaced*, which was also produced by Nira Park. *Black Books* features cameos by *Spaced* actors Simon Pegg, Nick Frost, Peter Serafinowicz and Jessica Stevenson.

2001 was not just a big year professionally for Freeman but also personally. It was when he met his long-term partner, actress Amanda Abbington, on the set of Channel 4's TV film *Men Only*. The two-part film, which was broadcast on 3 June in the UK, centres around five football players who rape a nurse on a horrible, ketamine-fuelled night and sees Freeman play a deeply unpleasant sex offender called Jamie.

Never too far from each other, Abbington later appeared in several more productions alongside Freeman, most notably *Sherlock*, *Swinging with the Finkels*, *The Debt* and *The All Together*.

Abbington spoke to the *Daily Mail*'s Vicki Power about seeing Freeman for the first time: 'I'd seen him in a TV sketch show and thought he was gorgeous. My ideal man. As I sat watching I said to my friend "He's lovely, isn't he? I'd love to meet him." Then a couple of months later I did.' One day, while in a make-up bus on the set of *Men Only*, she complained to her make-up girl that she didn't have a boyfriend, to which the make-up girl replied that there was a man on set who had been whining about a similar thing because he didn't have a girlfriend. 'At that minute Martin walked in and I just had a thunderbolt,' Abbington continued. 'It dawned on me, "Oh, God it's him!" We flirted with each other all day and when I went home he texted me, saying, "You left and I wasn't done flirting with you. That's a bit rude," which I thought was really smooth.' Freeman invited her out for a drink the next day and a few months later they were living together.

Following his appearance in *Men Only*, Freeman played various characters in five episodes of the seemingly now forgotten *World of Pub*. The comedy ran for six thirty-minute episodes from June to July of 2001 and was originally broadcast on BBC2. It had initially been a radio series that aired on Radio 4 from March 1998 to January 1999 and lasted for two series. It is set in an unpopular pub in London's East End and each episode ends up in a disaster of some sort.

The *British Comedy Guide* said, 'The series had previously run on BBC Radio 4 and did have some interesting ideas, but it did not have the legs to earn a second TV series. While the TV series was not successful, it did give some early TV appearances for future comedy stars including Peter Serafinowicz, Martin Freeman, Tamsin Greig and David Walliams.'

Total Film reviewed the DVD release and summarised, 'Cockney rhyming slang is well funny. But before you and the trouble and strife put up your plates for a butcher's at this 2001 sitcom featuring a pre-fame Martin Freeman, David Walliams and Tamsin Greig, pause a moment. Essentially a pub version of *Father Ted*, Tony Roche's wilfully silly show is one of the glut of early noughties comedies that hits just wide of the mark, complete with canned laughter echoing in the background.'

Freeman returned to the theatre in 1999 for a production of *La Dispute*, a staging of Pierre Marivaux's eighteenth-century play, co-produced by the RSC and Neil Bartlett's own Lyric Hammersmith, where the play was staged. Bartlett translated the original French and directed and designed the play, which, following its Hammersmith date on 15 April 1999, travelled north for showings in Brighton and Poole. Freeman won praise from critics for his performance as Azor. It was another string to his bow.

Martin Freeman's breakthrough TV role was undoubtedly the character of Tim Canterbury in *The Office*. He was dubious about going for the role initially because it was such a departure from what he'd done in the past but he reasoned that change is good, especially for a jobbing actor. He originally read for the part of Gareth, which ultimately went to Mackenzie Crook, and it was only as he was leaving the audition that Gervais offered him the part of Tim.

'There's a brilliant ordinariness to Martin's character, an endearing low-level grumpiness, and he was able to tap into that [in *The Office*],' said the show's producer, Ash Atalla, to *Guardian* journalist John Plunkett. 'He is a very charming, slightly grouchy man-next-door who has become a superstar.'

Freeman appeared in fourteen episodes of the acclaimed

series between 2001 and 2003. His first appearance was in the pilot and his last was in the *Christmas Special Part 2*, which aired on 27 December 2003. The *Christmas Specials* were hugely successful.

The Office has become one of the most popular and respected programmes in the history of British comedy on television. It was first broadcast on 9 July 2001 on BBC2 and, due to low ratings, it was almost cancelled. However, word of mouth and positive reviews gained it a consistent fan base. Entirely fictional and scripted, *The Office* was filmed in a documentary-style (often called 'mockumentary'), as the camera is acknowledged by the actors. It was created, written and directed by Ricky Gervais and Stephen Merchant and follows the day-to-day lives of a group of office employees in the Slough branch of the fictional Wernham Hogg Paper Company. Gervais plays the main character, David Brent, the office manager. A successful US remake ran from 2005 to 2013.

It is interesting that the Americans eventually took such a liking to *The Office* and decided to remake it. Often, US audiences can be very curious about non-home-grown TV shows, as they are an insular country by nature. They may know such shows as the detective drama series *Inspector Morse* or the comedy *Keeping Up Appearances* and a few others but these are set in lovely English towns and villages where everyone has a well-do-do accent. Americans know little – if anything – about the working class areas of Britain and the TV series that come out of it. Brits know about rock 'n' roll, jazz, blues, comic books, Hollywood movies and American TV but it's not something that is reciprocal. Americans know fewer

British TV shows. Also, America is so big that it could claim to know about *The Office* but perhaps it's only really New York and California and not the Mid-West or the South. Americans tend to take things they don't quite understand and totally remake them into something else they can comprehend. When Americans remake British films (*Get Carter*, *The Italian Job*) and TV shows (*Cracker*, *Prime Suspect*) the results are usually bad. *The Office US* only worked after season one because the writers made it something other than a literal remake of the original British version.

Freeman's personality suited the role of the straight man in *The Office*; he's an actor who has never begged to be liked or laughed at.

He explained to *IGN Filmforce*'s Ken P., 'I suppose the tone of *The Office* fits that, absolutely, and I guess that's why I'm in it – why they wanted me in it and why I wanted to be in it. Because it's so subtle, and that's the kind of sketch comedy I like. The Marx Brothers isn't subtle, and that's hilarious. There are a lot of things that aren't subtle but work just as well, but I think I'm best suited to stuff that is...'

Freeman's character in the show, Tim Canterbury, is a thirty-year-old sales representative whose sense of humour is very self-deprecating and ironic. He often jokes and flirts with the receptionist Dawn Tinsley (Lucy Davis). His office enemy is Gareth Kennan (Mackenzie Crook), whom Tim often plays practical jokes on to brighten up his otherwise tedious day. Tim, who seems to get along with everyone due to his sense of humour, humility and some good-natured traits, often jokes with his boss, David Brent, although their relationship has mixed results, as Brent is an extreme character with childlike behaviour and narcissism. However, Tim is something of a pathetic and insecure character who lives a shallow life. He lives with his parents and dropped out of university, only to end up in a job he feels no passion or zest for.

The flirtatious relationship between Tim and Dawn goes through several transitions throughout the series and becomes something of a 'will they/won't they' situation as the series progresses. However, Dawn is engaged to Lee (Joel Beckett), which prevents the work colleagues from deepening the feelings they have for each other. In the episode 'Training Day' Dawn and Lee have some relationship trouble, which Tim mistakenly believes means the end of their engagement, so he asks Dawn out and discovers that he was mistaken in his assumption. Tim jumps to his own defence by saying that he was only asking her out 'as friends'. Tim and Dawn seem to drift apart during series two, especially as Tim gets a promotion and begins to take his job more seriously. He starts to date Rachel, a former Swindon employee. It's obvious that Dawn becomes jealous over his new relationship and even his nemesis Gareth is jealous because he had feelings for Rachel before she started going out with Tim.

During the fifth episode of the second series, Dawn sells kisses for Red Nose Day and Tim makes a donation and they kiss. He is torn between his feelings for both Dawn and Rachel but he is not aware that Dawn and Lee plan to move to the US. Tim breaks up with Rachel and admits to Dawn his feelings for her but his confession is kept private from the cameras as he takes his mic off. Both characters are left depressed by the end of the series.

As time passes, Tim becomes unhappy in his job, while Dawn and Lee are equally unhappy living in Florida. They fly back for the office reunion and she reignites her friendship with Tim. They finally become a couple after she receives a Christmas present from Tim telling her to hold on to her dream of becoming an illustrator. She returns to the Christmas party without Lee.

The Office was an accurate representation of Freeman's sardonic sense of humour, although he admitted to *Dark Horizon*'s Paul Fischer that he also adores old-school slapstick comedy: 'It was certainly pretty close,' he said in the interview. 'I mean, my taste in humour does go from slapping you around the face in *Tom and Jerry*, to *The Office*, Larry Sanders, or to Harold Lloyd, from the silly to the clever. I love physical shtick, and all sorts of things that are done well.'

Freeman was nominated for Best Comedy Actor at the 2002 British Comedy Awards and then nominated for a BAFTA at the 2004 awards for Best Comedy Performance for his role in *The Office Christmas Specials*, for which he also won a British Comedy Award nomination.

'I don't like affectation,' he said to *Esquire*'s Michael Holden in 2012. 'I think my job is to help tell the story and anything else is just showing off, trying to win awards and I truly do think that's silly.'

No one knew *The Office* was going to be so successful and have such an impact on modern popular culture. Freeman thoroughly enjoyed his time in *The Office* and said he knew from the minute he saw the rough cut that it was going to be a great series: 'It's a funny thing, *The Office*, because millions and millions and millions and millions of people didn't watch it,' he said to the *Washington Post*'s Alona Wartofsky. 'But culturally, it is more of a phenomenon than almost anything else I can remember as far as British television is concerned.

'I think it had a bit more guts than other shows that have gone into that format,' he added. 'It was more uncomfortable to watch than a lot of things on television are.'

The Office had picked up some famous fans. On a trip to LA – his first visit to Hollywood – for the Golden Globes in 2004, he met Harry Shearer and Christopher Guest of *This Is Spinal Tap*. '… how many people do they meet and say, "Oh, I loved your show"?' Freeman said to *The Guardian*'s Stephanie Merritt. 'I mean, I heard that Paul McCartney always taped *The Office*, but that doesn't mean he feels the same way about me that I feel about the Beatles.'

His first trip to Hollywood freaked him out. He felt like it was its own planet, alien to the rest of the US, let alone the world. Hollywood represents fantasy; it is a world of its own making. Freeman is English and he loves London and his family and does not wish to pursue an LA lifestyle. One would imagine that life in LA can be very emotional. 'If I began to like it out there, I'd think I was going mad,' he admitted to Andrew Duncan of *Reader's Digest*, 'rather than chilling out and not having a chip on my shoulder. I give myself chips. It's my way of keeping myself in check. There's a streak in me that says, "Life is not all great. Keep vigilant".'

An intensely private man, Freeman shied away from the red-carpet events and all the glitz and glamour hoopla that came with his new celebrity lifestyle, choosing to stay at home with his family. He preferred to concentrate on the art of acting and the many technical details that come with it and avoid becoming trapped in the whirlwind lifestyle that fame and fortune brought him on the back of *The Office*. He admitted that he struggled to cope with the recognition that came with the series' success. Some people apparently even thought he was an office worker before he appeared in the series and had no idea that he was an experienced actor who had several years of professional work behind him. 'Have you done anything else?' he would get asked by curious members of the public.

Freeman told the *Daily Express*'s Cheryl Stonehouse, 'You soon realise you should never take that adulation seriously. People called me a legend but what they really meant was that they'd seen me on the telly. Some people moan about the cult of celebrity but if these people don't want to be photographed then they should stay in.'

The role seemed to be a blessing and a curse for Freeman: in one way it opened his career up to new roles and made him a TV star but on the flip side, in the eyes of the public, it looked as though he was always going to be Tim Canterbury, and he struggled to get away from that stereotype. It is a predicament that many actors face when they are specifically associated with one role. Some actors never get away from their first or most popular character, no matter how hard they try; others attempt to completely turn their career around. Martin Freeman was desperate to get away from the tag 'the bloke who played Tim in *The Office*'.

'… obviously I don't want to be seen as that character for the rest of my life – I'd like it to be seen as one of a number of things I'm proud to have done,' Freeman admitted to *The Guardian*'s Stephanie Merritt in 2004. 'But then I'm proud of plays I did in front of 200 people that no one gives a shit about who wasn't there, and that doesn't negate it for me.'

There often comes a point when certain members of the public assume the actor is the character they play and, as a result, they sometimes think they know that person off-screen but, of course, it is not the case.

'If I leave the house it happens every day,' Freeman said to *Metro*'s Andrew Williams. 'I wasn't dragged up, so I know how to be polite and how to speak to people. People think they know you. There are similarities between me and Tim but I am not him. If it means something to someone, that's good – we didn't make the show for people to feel indifferent about it. I am glad it's affected people but there are times if you're at a gig or a club and someone slaps you on the back and it's not good. I tell them off if I think they've gone over the line.'

There was one point where Freeman admits the fame may have got to him and he started to develop an ego, which is understandable. Both he and his partner Amanda were jobbing actors with steady pay cheques coming in and, all of a sudden, people were nudging Amanda out of the way so they could speak to Freeman.

'That is going to make her feel even more insecure and make me look like I'm being an arrogant prick,' Freeman said to the *Observer*'s Andrew Anthony. 'I'm not saying I wasn't an arrogant prick. If I was, she says it didn't last long.'

Freeman has never had any inclination to see a return of *The Office*. His blueprint for the series is the classic British comedy *Fawlty Towers*, which ran for just two series consisting of twelve episodes yet, decades later, is still thought of as one of the all-time great comedy shows.

'I think *The Office* was the right length,' Freeman said to *ShortList* in 2014. 'A huge reason it's so beloved is that we left it. And I think on the one hand people say, "I wish you'd done more," and I think, "Well you might wish that now, but in five years you might not be thinking that when you're saying, 'Oh it's not as good as it used to be,'" and I always admired Ricky and Steve for calling it a day.'

None of the cast and creative team expected to make so much money from the DVD sales of the series. 'No one could have dreamed it would become a cultural phenomenon,' Freeman said to BBC Movies' Rob Carnevale. 'We were doing it because it was really good and we really liked it. And if only seven people had liked it, I'd still be dead proud of it.'

One thing that Freeman remembers from the set of *The Office* is the light-hearted theological debates with Ricky Gervais. Freeman, a Catholic, and Gervais, known to be an atheist, would talk about the many concerns relating to religion, but those talks never got too serious.

Freeman has since admitted he would like to work with Gervais again but it has, to date, never been on the cards. He has also stated that such a reunion of the old gang would, perhaps, not be a wise move as he has tried so hard to move away from his character in *The Office*. Martin has always had the guts to move on from any role he has been associated with. He's not an actor who likes to live off past glories but rather one who looks ahead to other roles and new ventures.

It was not surprising that some of his *Office* colleagues went to America for work but Freeman remained a steadfastly London-based actor.

'It really depends on what it is,' he said to *IGN*'s Leigh Singer, when asked about his choice of roles. 'It genuinely does because of course some big American films are absolutely brilliant and some of them aren't, but that's the way of everything. I don't write anything off without reading a script and if it's a good one, I'll consider it, whether it's for twenty dollars or a million dollars.'

The Office was not a full-time gig, so Freeman had other roles to branch out with. He cropped up as a pirate in the film *Fancy Dress*, written and directed by Jon Wright and released on 21 November 2001, and he had various other bit parts as well.

Once *The Office* became a success, Freeman reasoned that he was on a train that was not going to slow down and he was right: the scripts came flying through his door. But that did not mean he wasn't insecure, as many actors are. He understood what a fickle business he was in and that one year you could be inundated with scripts, only to struggle to find work months later. Actors are never completely safe: the industry might tell you you're the next Robert DeNiro but a year later slap you in the face, throw cold water at you and tell you your career is over and you're relegated to TV movies.

He was cast as Richard 'Ricky C' Cunningham in the 2002 comedy *Ali G Indahouse*, based on the popular Channel 4 series by writer, actor and comedian Sacha Baron Cohen. Usually, comedy series work less well on the big screen than they do on TV but *Ali G Indahouse* was relatively successful, receiving some modest reviews and reasonable box-office returns. The film, which was released on 22 March 2002, also stars Michael Gambon as the Prime Minister, Charles Dance as the Deputy Prime Minister and Kellie Bright as Ali G's love interest, Julie.

Total Film said of Ali G's big-screen adventure, 'It isn't going to redefine British comedy, it lacks the satirical bite of Ali G's best work and there's no chance of selling it to the Americans, but Cohen has just about pulled it off. In the lowest-brow way possible, of course.'

CHAPTER FOUR

THE DRAMATIC ACTOR

'Some people like me, and you either have a thing that
people want to follow or you don't.'
FREEMAN SPEAKING TO ALICE WIGNALL IN
THE GUARDIAN, 2009

With the success of *The Office*, people saw Freeman as a comedy actor. This was a notion he chose to squash as he began to shift his career towards more dramatic roles on TV.

From 18 April to 11 May 2002 Freeman returned to the theatre to star in *Kosher Harry* at London's Royal Court. Directed by comedienne and actress Kathy Burke, written by Nick Grosso and co-starring Mark Benton, Claudie Blakley and June Watson, the play focuses on the racism that occurs in London life and how it has continued with each passing generation. It is set in a kosher café in St John's Wood, where Russian waitresses are called 'Gladiola' because their names are considered unpronounceable by the locals, all the Jews are in show business, black people eat only banana fritters and the Spanish have a weak moral backbone. The play centres on the characters that frequent the café.

Philip Fisher wrote in the *British Theatre Guide*, 'As might be expected from a play written by Nick Grosso and directed by Kathy Burke, there is a real hard edge to the comedy. Not one of the four characters is what he or she seems to be and the central figure, a young man played nonchalantly by the excellent Martin Freeman, might even be a servant of Beelzebub. The play is made up of a number of short scenes containing perfect-sounding dialogue that often has limited meaning. These scenes are split by one-second explosions rather like instant power cuts.'

The Independent's Rhoda Koenig slammed the play, however: '*Kosher Harry* makes a point of locating its restaurant in St John's Wood, a prosperous Jewish neighbourhood in London. There is only one such establishment there, and I wouldn't like anyone to think there's a connection, for its service and hygiene are far superior and its customers funnier than those shown here. Is *Kosher Harry* the worst play of 2002? I'd like to think so, but there's only so much optimism I can summon up.'

Maddy Costa wrote in her three out of five-star review in *The Guardian*, 'In Kathy Burke's nifty production in the Royal Court's Theatre Upstairs, the play is intermittently hilarious, unnerving and trapped in Pinter's shadow. The performances are excellent: Claudie Blakley struts winningly as the waitress, June Watson finds a singularity in the caricatured old woman, and Mark Benton is a wonderfully crude cabbie. Martin Freeman is particularly good as the man, his face moulding itself constantly to mirror the thoughts of his companions. Like Burke, the cast revel in the grotesque cockney banter; they bring a farcical tone to the evening, but never the intensity that the play needs to really resonate.'

Dominic Cavendish penned a review in the *Daily Telegraph*, saying, 'Kathy Burke – who has been turning from acting to directing of late – elicits buoyant, attention-seeking performances from her cast but can't disguise the play's sagging credibility. A tottering catastrophe of smudged lipstick and pigtails, Claudie Blakley's waitress is almost a duplicate version of Burke at her trashiest hilarious best, even doing those signature curtseying movements. And Mark Benton is a thoroughly convincing fat-gut, no-brained cabbie. As the young stranger, Martin Freeman, the terminally bored hero of the BBC sitcom *The Office* – fidgets at [his] table, eyebrows working overtime to convey polite interest in the natter. You can tell, though, that he'd rather be anywhere else. And who can blame him?'

Freeman later starred as DC Stone in three episodes of the British legal drama *Helen West* in 2002. Based on three books by acclaimed crime author Frances Fyfield, *Helen West* stars Amanda Burton as a crown prosecutor with a deep passion for the legal system and who is particularly interested in women's issues.

ITV piloted *Helen West* as a one-off episode in 1999 starring Juliet Stevensen but the actress didn't want to commit herself to an ongoing series and declined to return. ITV subsequently hired *Silent Witness* actress Amanda Burton for the drama, which cost a staggering £3 million to make. The channel was looking for a crime series to replace *Kavanagh QC*, which starred the late *Inspector Morse* actor John Thaw. Alan Wright, the chief executive of the series's producers, Arrowhead, spoke to BBC News Online about *Helen West*: 'It's a character we hope will find favour with the audience. As with all these things, its future will be determined by ratings… But it has been consciously designed as a returning series.'

Freeman first appeared in the episode 'Deep Sleep', which aired on 6 May 2002. He then appeared in 'Shadow Play', which was broadcast on 13 May, and 'A Clear Conscience', which aired on 20 May.

He also played the character of Matt in an episode in series two of *Linda Green* entitled 'Easy Come, Easy Go', which aired on 10 December 2002. *Linda Green* ran for two series between 2001 and 2002 and was originally broadcast on BBC1. The series focuses on its namesake (played by Lisa Tarbuck), a thirty-something woman whose day job is that of a car sales woman who works as a club singer at night. The series follows the issues of love, relationships and friends and features appearances from Christopher Eccleston, David Morrissey, Simon Pegg, Pam Ferris, Anne Reid, Jamie Theakston, Peter Kay and Meera Syal in addition to Martin Freeman. Ratings slipped, however, and a third series was not commissioned.

The series received very mixed reviews. Gareth McLean of *The Guardian* was unenthused: 'I really wanted to like *Linda Green*… And yet, it was ill-conceived, dramatically unsatisfying and a huge disappointment… When your standards are high, your reputation formidable and your output 10 times better than anything your peers are producing, it is much easier to disappoint your audience.'

Robert Hanks of *The Independent* wrote, 'The combination of Abbott's needling, believable dialogue and Tarbuck's sharply timed delivery is appealing… but, despite the hype, *Linda Green* isn't breaking any new ground… Her sassy, witty person isn't a million miles from the character Lesley Sharp played in Abbott's *Clocking Off*.'

The *Daily Mirror*'s Tony Purnell said, '*Linda Green* should be the perfect combination for a comedy drama but it turns out to be a very uneasy mix... It was much cruder and far less funny than *Cold Feet* or *Coupling*.'

Paul Connolly wrote in *The Times*, 'Very quickly, the serrated script, perspicacious observations and well-drawn cast of characters draw you in.'

Following his appearance in *Linda Green*, Freeman was cast as Terry Ross in the TV film *The Debt*, about a former robber who agrees, albeit reluctantly, to do one more robbery to protect his family. Freeman's character is the less-than-useful son-in-law of retired safe-breaker Geoff Dresner, played by seasoned TV actor Warren Clarke. Released on 21 August 2003, *The Debt* also stars Hugo Speer and Freeman's partner Amanda Abbington. Much of the film's story is told in flashbacks and offers a somewhat muddled chronology of events.

'*The Debt* is a story about a criminal, a detective and a lawyer and how their lives collide with each other,' explained writer Richard McBrien to BBC News. 'The idea is that all three men owe debts to their children in some way which affects the way they do their job.

'I can sympathise with all three characters,' continues McBrien. 'I wanted to show that in their own world, criminals, detectives and lawyers are all good people, not real villains. The there [*sic*] men are trying to lead a good life but become compromised by events.'

Freeman continued his ventures into more dramatic roles

when he played D.S. Stringer in the 2003 TV film *Margery And Gladys*, which was broadcast on 21 September of that year. It also stars Penelope Keith, June Brown and Roger Lloyd-Pack. The story concerns the recently widowed Margery Heywood (Keith) and her cleaning lady Gladys Gladwell (Brown), who interrupt a man breaking into Margery's home in Kent. She attacks the man with a heavy glass vase, which knocks him unconscious. She suspects he is dead, panics and departs the house with Gladys but leaves behind her handbag. The two women decide to drive to Margery's son, Graham, who lives in Milton Keynes, hoping for money and shelter. The trip turns into a comedy of errors as they are forced to break into a chemist to get some insulin for Gladys's diabetes. The story follows them as they try to evade police attention and CCTV cameras while Margery discovers a twenty-year affair between her late husband and Gladys, which her son was aware of. The film ends on a night out in Blackpool, where the two women board a boat to the Caribbean. It was directed by Geoffrey Sax, who later made his cinematic debut with the 2005 horror flick *White Noise*. It is fun, harmless TV-film fodder aimed at older audiences.

The Guardian's Nancy Banks-Smith observed, 'They [Margery and Gladys] are pursued by police and press: the deafening Martin Freeman ('OK! Listen up! Big breakthrough!'), a characterisation, I feel, based on the glorious DCI Grim in *The Thin Blue Line*; the laconic Lloyd-Pack; and the salivating "Scoop" Morley.'

The Sydney Morning Herald's Robin Oliver wrote of the film, 'Some nice cameos here – Peter Vaughan as Gladys's husband, Troy, and Roger Lloyd-Pack (*The Vicar Of Dibley*) as Detective Inspector Woolley. *Margery & Gladys* doesn't hold a candle to *The Norman Conquests*, but it provides pleasing Saturday night fare.'

Despite his switch to more serious roles in that year, Freeman still found time for comedy. On 14 March 2003 *Comic Relief 2003: The Big Hair Do* was screened. It featured the finest of British comedy talent, including Lenny Henry, Jonathan Ross, Harry Enfield and Rowan Atkinson. Martin Freeman starred as Johnny Rotten in a *Blankety Blank* sketch.

Freeman was continuing to balance his acting talents with both comedy and dramatic parts. However, many of his film roles were little more than cameos. He starred as John in Richard Curtis's successful 2003 romantic comedy *Love Actually*: a film set in London at Christmas time that follows ten separate stories, each showing the many different aspects of love. As the film progresses, the stories become interlinked. The film is played out in a weekly countdown five weeks before Christmas and concludes with an epilogue one month later. Released on 21 November 2003, *Love Actually* was an enormous financial success worldwide and received positive reviews from critics. The ensemble cast includes such revered British actors as Alan Rickman, Emma Thompson, Hugh Grant, Keira Knightley, Colin Firth, Liam Neeson, Bill Nighy and Rowan Atkinson.

Freeman plays John, a professional body double. He meets his partner Judy (Joanna Page), also a body double, on the set of a hardcore porn film. They appear to be very natural in front of the camera performing penetrative sex but off-screen they are very coy around each other. They endeavour to pursue a relationship together and attend the Christmas pageant at the local school with John's brother. The ten stories interweave and draw a final conclusion.

On appearing nude, Freeman told the *Washington Post*'s Alona Wartofsky, 'It's hard to be naked in front of 150 people. It's not in any way pleasant. As a man it gives you a kind of window of what quite a lot of jobs are like for quite a lot of women.'

Love Actually was nominated for Best Cast at the Phoenix Film Critics Society awards as well as Best Acting Ensemble at the Critics' Choice Movie Awards. The team bagged the award for Best Ensemble Cast at the Washington DC Area Film Critics Association Awards.

Peter Bradshaw was unenthusiastic about the film, giving it two out of five stars in his review in *The Guardian* but he praised the cast: 'Hugh Grant is always good value, and Martin Freeman and Joanna Page do very well as a couple who fall in love while working as stand-ins for what is apparently an expensively produced hardcore porn film.'

Writing in the *Daily Telegraph*, Sukhdev Sandhu said, 'It's the newer faces, many imported from television, that offer the greatest pleasures. Gregor Fisher as the doting manager of Bill Nighy, a foul-mouthed has-been rocker who is trying to revive his career. Martin Freeman, from *The Office*, as a mild-mannered porn actor who falls for his equally sweet co-star; Andrew Lincoln, from *This Life* and *Teachers*, gives a performance that at times recalls John Cusack.'

Freeman also portrayed Lord Shaftesbury in the acclaimed BBC2 TV mini-series *Charles II: The Power and The Passion*, which was filmed in Prague in the Czech Republic and broadcast in November 2003.

'It wasn't just about the wigs and the tights, as if that legitimises you as an actor,' Freeman said to *The Guardian*'s Stephanie Merritt. 'I try very hard not to be flattered or bamboozled by money into doing anything, I turned stuff down when I was signing on if I didn't think it was something I'd be proud of. But if it's a good script and a good story, then by Christ, bring on the wigs!'

The film stars Rufus Sewell, Martin Turner and Ian McDiarmid and was written by award-winner Adrian Hodges. The creative team aimed to make the story, which tells of Charles II's tenure on the throne, his decade long exile from England during the reign of Oliver Cromwell and his triumphant return to England, as historically accurate as possible.

Writer Adrian Hodges told BBC News, 'I found a character in Charles himself who struck me as immensely modern, someone who could speak to us now about the ageless issues of personal and public morality, love, sex, hate, fear, anger and death.'

A heavily edited version was aired in the US under the title *The Last King: The Power And The Passion Of King Charles II*. Both versions were produced by the BBC in association with the American A&E Network.

'I think the key to him is that he was constantly shifting and his sole belief was to keep the crown as it was the one thing he promised to his father,' Rufus Sewell explained to BBC News of King Charles II. 'So he was capable of being compassionate but also cold and calculating.'

Freeman's role in the film appeared to go unnoticed but it

received some positive reviews when it was released on DVD. *The Guardian*'s Rupert Smith wrote of the original broadcast, 'This really was history as drama, with all that implies; it was also one of the very few dramas this year that I wanted to watch without being paid to do so. If *Charles II* can be topped, I'll eat my full-bottomed wig.'

DVD Verdict's Amanda DeWees wrote of the US edit, 'Structured in two parts, the film is dogged by an episodic structure, which may have been worsened by edits: The British version of the film clocks in at about four hours, which means that almost an hour of footage was cut from this release. These cuts would go some way toward explaining why the first half of the film sometimes seems like a choppy succession of similar scenes: politicians in shouting matches, lovers in wrestling matches, and various characters bursting into rooms to throw hissy fits. The second half of the film recovers to some extent from the episodic beginning and gains some unity of story through the unfolding of the Popish Plot. Likewise, this part seems to find the heart of the story and the characters, where the first half was more concerned with their political lives.'

Freeman took on varying roles to challenge himself as an actor and, in part, to challenge the public's perception, however misguided, of him as some sort of everyday chap. He is proud to appear in art-house films and less commercial features because they reflect his personal tastes.

'I'm not purely benign, yeah,' Freeman admitted to *Esquire*'s Michael Holden in 2012. 'I mean – I know I'm not, no one fucking is, but people want to just say… you know, I can name other actors who – I won't – but you could think of a thousand other actors who people wouldn't feel, "Oh, would you say hello to my mum?" because people would be a bit scared to do that. But with me I've played the parts where people think, "He's just a good bloke".

Freeman had been acting for well over a decade but there were only a couple of things he was best known for at this particular juncture.

'So what people mean when they say I'm likable is this and *The Office*, or *Love Actually*,' he said to the BBC's Alana Lee. 'Again, you can't answer it without sounding defensive or chippy, but I've virtually not had any time out in a decade. My first forays into telly were as sort of drug-taking rent boys who didn't know whether to fuck you or kill you. They were all these kind of people and it was, like, "Oh, he's got an edge, this guy Martin." Now the cycle turns, and it's, "Oh, he's so lovely."'

Despite Freeman's wish not to be typecast as Tim Canterbury from *The Office*, he does accept that he's been fairly lucky in moving away from the character through more recent roles. 'I think people now know that I'm not just Tim from *The Office*. The only place that image persists is with a few lazy journalists. You'll sometimes see a picture of me in something like *Charles II* with the caption "Tim from *The Office* in a funny wig". I'd like you to apologise for that on behalf of the NUJ,' he told *The Independent*'s James Rampton in 2007.

Freeman was glad to have moved on to other projects. There was so much that he wanted to do as an actor and he refused to be limited to *The Office* and comedy in general.

He told BBC Radio 5 Live presenter Richard Bacon in an interview in 2014, 'I'm very proud of *The Office*. If it's on, I still watch it and will laugh. But one of the best things Ricky and Steve did was ending it and making it finite and making it something people look back [on] and go, "I wish there was more of that," as opposed to doing loads and people saying, "I wish there was less of this."'

He added, 'I'm glad not to be doing *The Office* anymore, not for any career reason or any selfish reason but as a punter, just as a viewer. I'm glad we're not ruining it.'

Next up on the small screen, he was cast as Mike in the two-series sitcom *Hardware*, which aired between 2003 and 2004 and ran for a full twelve episodes.

'There are people who wonder why I did it, and it's hard not to sound chippy, but it made me laugh,' Freeman explained to *The Guardian*'s Stephanie Merritt in 2004. 'People might think that there's something boring about it because it's a much more traditional ITV studio sitcom, but for me it was pure affection for the show – I can say I know why I did it and that's what matters. There's this misunderstanding, too – because it didn't get as much attention – but far more people watch *Hardware* than ever saw *The Office*, just by dint of it being on ITV.'

The series also starred Peter Serafinowicz, Ken Morley, Ryan Cartwright, Susan Earl and Ella Kenion. It was written and created by Simon Nye, the man behind the hugely popular sitcom *Men Behaving Badly*. The programme is set in Harnway's Hardware Store in London, where Mike works with Steve (Ryan Cartwright) and Kenny (Peter Serafinowicz) for shop owner Rex. Next door but one there is a café called Nice Day Café, where Mike's girlfriend Anne (Susan Earl) works with Julie (Ella Kenion). The series basically revolves around the staff of the hardware store as they make fun of the DIY fanatics that frequent the premises. The role bagged Freeman the Best Male Comedy Performance award at the 2004 European Rose d'Or awards.

'You think, how do I get out of this? and the answer is I can't,' he said to Alice Wignall of *The Guardian* when talking about choosing projects. 'Even if I think I don't want to do comedy for ages, if I read a script and it's really good, I want to do it.'

However, Freeman quit the series to pursue serious acting roles, wanting to turn his back on comedy. *Hardware* was a critical failure but it pulled in around four million viewers. If his heart's not really in it, Freeman finds it difficult to enjoy the work. He was concerned by the notion that he may be seen as a sitcom actor when his talents extend far beyond half-an-hour weekly episodes of British TV.

'He wants to turn his back on comedy to avoid typecasting,' a source told the *Sun* at the time of the series, in 2004. 'ITV comedy chiefs are now looking to cast another actor or comedian in his role [in *Hardware*].'

Freeman later spoke to *ShortList* about *Hardware*: '… y'know I stopped doing it after two series – I didn't want to do it anymore. You're either hardwired to think in that *Fawlty Towers* way or you're not... and I think you can think, "Oh let's keep going until we get into syndication and make pots of money or whatever" – and of course I like money – but I prefer leaving something behind that people go, "That was the right length."'

2003 brought some notable roles for Freeman and with it came a certain degree of fame and public acknowledgement.

Freeman has often struggled with fame as a concept. He doesn't especially enjoy the trappings that it brings, preferring instead to focus his energy elsewhere. He criticised reality television and said in 2003 that we have reached the zenith of people becoming famous without talent.

'You know, apparently when Noël Coward met The Beatles he was very nice to them and said to other people, "They're completely talentless,"' Freeman explained to the *Observer*'s Andrew Anthony in 2014. 'He was older than I am now but still, you've got to be careful about what you write off because you can be so solid in your knowledge. You don't want to be the person who said the Beatles are talentless.'

He reiterated his opinions on modern-day society's obsession with celebrity culture and how it is out of control to *The Independent*'s James Rampton in 2007: 'These days it's not enough to be acknowledged as a surgeon – you have to be acknowledged as the cover-star of *Grazia* magazine. After all, that's much more valuable to society than saving a child's life, isn't it?'

Freeman isn't interested in the celebrity life at all. He certainly doesn't want to make a career out of it and tends to wonder, with any celebrity event he goes to – which are few and far between and generally part of the promotional work for something he is acting in – why people make a fuss about him. Usually, he sees celebrity events as a waste of time. He'd rather be at home with his family.

'I thought actors were dodgy until I hung out with stand-up comedians,' he admitted to Andrew Duncan of *Reader's Digest*. 'They're pathologically egotistical and make us seem like selfless wallflowers by comparison. I don't want to be around people who can't shut up. I guess they're insecure, but isn't everyone – unless you're mental or boring?'

Though it was only a cameo, Freeman was cast as Declan in the zombie film *Shaun of the Dead*, released on 9 April 2004. The film is the first in the *Three Flavours Cornetto Trilogy* by actors Simon Pegg, Nick Frost and director Edgar Wright and inspired by George A. Romero's revered *Dead* trilogy. *Shaun of the Dead* sees Pegg play Shaun, a man who attempts to deal with the issues of his life – namely his girlfriend and his mother and stepfather – while battling an apocalyptic uprising of zombies. The film is filled with pop-culture references, most notably to movies, TV shows and video games. The film is, in many ways, similar to the TV series *Spaced*, which Pegg, Frost and Wright co-created. *Shaun of the Dead* was, in actual fact, inspired by the *Spaced* episode 'Art', which sees Pegg's character Tim hallucinate that he is fighting a zombie invasion under the influence of amphetamines and the PlayStation video game *Resident Evil 2*. *Shaun of the Dead* features several actors from *Spaced*, *Black Books* and *The Office*, including Dylan Moran (*Black Books*), Tamsin Greig (*Black Books*), Julia Deakin (*Spaced*) and Reece Shearsmith (*Spaced*).

Filmed over nine weeks in May and July of 2003, the comedy film received rave reviews from critics and picked up some famous fans along the way, such as Quentin Tarantino, Stephen King and George A. Romero. It was a box-office success and became an instant cult classic.

Empire's horror-film expert and author Kim Newman said of the film, 'A surprisingly good TV transfer for the *Spaced* crew.

It may not exactly be Ealing, but it's funny for long stretches. Even when in danger of self-destructing, it cadges laughs with smart lines, silly observations or blokish inside jokes about zombie movies, video games and pub nibbles.'

2004 also saw Freeman cast as Fleck in the TV film *Pride*, written by Simon Nye and released on 27 December. The film is about two lion cubs as they grow up and face adult life. Computer-generated imagery was used with digital effects by the esteemed Jim Henson's Creature Shop. It was shot in Tanzania's Serengeti National Park and, aside from Freeman, it features the voices of Kate Winslet (Suki), Sean Bean (Dark), Helen Mirren (Macheeba), Jim Broadbent (Eddie), Robbie Coltrane (James), Rupert Graves (Linus), John Hurt (Harry) and Kwame Kwei-Armah (Lush). It was produced by the BBC and broadcast on the A&E station in the US.

Freeman was next seen as Kevin in the film *Call Register*. In the film, Kevin wants to get in touch with a girl he met recently named Amanda (Neve McIntosh), so he borrows his best mate Julian's (James Lance) phone. When he dials Amanda's number, the phone recognises the number and identifies her by name, which means Julian knows Amanda. Kevin arranges a date with her and learns that she'd once dated Julian and had slept with him, which understandably makes Kevin feel uncomfortable. The film then follows a series of phone calls between the three characters.

Yahoo's Contributing Network writer Philo Gabriel praised the film, saying, 'In any case, it's a winner. If you appreciate this style of humour at all, it's worth checking out.'

Freeman continued to explore more diverse parts. He played

Vila in the 2005 short comedy film *Blake's Junction 7*, which follows the cult 1980s science-fiction gang Blake's 7 as they make a lively late-night stop at Newport Pagnell Services on the M1 motorway.

The actor explained to *Empire*, 'It's not that I don't love comedy and don't want to do comedy, but my background isn't in comedy. If I do comedy for too long, and nothing else, then it'll just look like I'm trying to validate myself by playing a child killer, or whatever. Whereas, actually, that's always been quite natural to me, to play straight things.'

Freeman received another big break with his portrayal of hapless protagonist Arthur Dent in the 2005 film *The Hitchhiker's Guide to the Galaxy*, released on 28 April of that year. This was his first major Hollywood role. Many actors had been attached to the portrayal of Arthur Dent over the years but it was Freeman who the creative team had in mind. He didn't fight for the role, because that's not his style.

'At first I didn't think I'd get the part but when I thought about it, I reckoned maybe I was right,' Freeman told the *Daily Mail*'s Chris Sullivan in 2008. 'Arthur had to be believed and I suppose I have that rooted quality, someone you can side with, which isn't a bad thing.'

After the script arrived, Freeman met with the director and producer and did a reading for them. They had told him which scenes to prepare and the reading went well and, from there, he worked with director Garth Jennings on developing the role.

'People feel a sense of ownership with this story – particularly this person – because he's the last [surviving] human,' Freeman told AP Radio. 'I'm aware of some people thinking I was a really great choice [to play him] and some people thinking I was a terrible choice.'

He reiterated this to *Movie Web*'s Julian Roman: 'I knew some people would think I was a great idea and some would think I was a terrible idea. And I know that's still the case. All I can do is just do what I can do and not be hampered by knowing that some people won't like it. But some people won't like everything I do.'

Freeman wasn't a fan of the series of books, as such, though his family had the novels at home and while he'd read them he was not fanatically enthusiastic. He thought *The Hitchhiker's Guide to the Galaxy* was a good story and one that was perfect for the big screen. It wasn't the role he had been waiting decades to play and nor was it something that he was especially destined to act, but he was more than capable of pulling it off. Dent is the main character and the one the audience root for because he is the last man on Earth, so Freeman's character is the film's most important role.

When he read the books for research and preparation, Freeman appreciated Adams's irreverent, dry and sarcastic sense of humour and the fact that Adams never censored himself. The late British author had his ideas and was willing to go where the story took him, even if it meant the other side of the universe. There's some silly schoolboy humour amongst Adams's work, which became a trademark of his, but the perceived frivolousness did not mask the story's inherent intelligence.

Freeman approached the role the only way he knew how, which was not to mimic Simon Jones, who had played Dent in the original 1981 TV series, but rather to look at the script in an objective way and to play the part in the best way he could, using the details of the script.

'...I just played it as real and as funnily as possible, all the while knowing that you're in a comedy,' Martin explained to *LatinoReview*. 'You've got to kind of know what you're in. So it's slightly heightened with humour. The humour is definitely there, but I thought that the stakes had to be genuine because he's a man whose day starts badly, and within ten minutes of the film, his planet's gone. So all of his reference points, every single thing that he's ever known or thought he knew or will ever know has gone.'

The filming process was laborious because it was necessary for Freeman to wear a thick dressing gown throughout the summer, as seen in the film. The days were long and hot. On top of that, Martin was envious of Mos Def's and Zooey Deschanel's attire, feeling unglamorous in comparison. The young actor got along really well with Mos Def – they spoke about music the whole time. Freeman also found him very easy to work with and considered Mos to be an all-round 'top bloke'.

Working on *The Hitchhiker's Guide to the Galaxy* was a different experience for Freeman because it was a much bigger-scale production than anything he had worked on previously. He had a sense that there was a lot of money floating around because of the film sets, and there was a much bigger crew than he was used to and more people around on set. He enjoyed getting lifts in nice cars to and from the location each day and there was more choice on the menu when it was time to eat. Coming from a background in British TV and theatre, this was the sort of service he was unused to. The one thing that he found was a bit of a drag was the boredom that sinks in in-between shoots because organising sets takes longer for films than for TV.

Much of the film's cast is American, though the books are British and it was filmed in London with a British crew, yet Freeman felt like the only Brit on set at times.

'I think people's fear – well certainly British people's fear – is that it would be completely Hollywoodized or morphed into this thing where the stuff we initially cared about is no longer there,' he explained to *Movie Web*'s Julian Roman. 'I believe and hope people don't feel that's happened. Occasionally I would feel like the only Limey in town. I felt it was in good hands. No one was on board to scuttle it. They all wanted to serve the film and make something good happen. We were all on the same side.'

To his ongoing frustration, Freeman is seen as the everyday British man. Dent is not written as a hero or a screen icon in the vein of James Bond. He's the last surviving human and just an average, flawed bloke. He has a job he isn't enamoured by and has little luck with women. These are things many men can relate too. Freeman just wanted to be real and funny, that's all. A great deal was riding on him as the main character and linchpin of the story.

'I could pretend to be posh, but I didn't think there was any point really,' Freeman confessed to *Empire*. 'I think, maybe, having the last surviving person from Earth be very upper middle class and probably went to Cambridge wasn't as accessible as having someone who doesn't look or sound like they did that stuff. So Sam [Rockwell] probably means it as a compliment because I guess he thinks we hit it more on the head by going for that.'

Freeman did not see any connection between Tim Canterbury and Arthur Dent, though he was asked about it multiple times in interviews. There is a real sense of wonder with Dent at what he is seeing in the universe, which Freeman wonderfully enacts with his facial characteristics and mannerisms. The scene where Slartibartfast takes Dent around the planet factory is especially effective in this regard.

When Martin was asked by the BBC's Alana Lee if he saw any similarities between Arthur Dent and Tim Canterbury, he responded, 'I think because I'm doing it people see that. I think if Hugh Bonneville was playing it they wouldn't say, "He was a bit like Tim from *The Office*." But I am using the same vocal cords and the same ears for both parts so I'm not going to be cast as many 70-year-old black women.'

The Hitchhiker's Guide to the Galaxy also stars Sam Rockwell as Zaphod Beeblebrox, Mos Def as Ford Prefect, Zooey Deschanel as Tricia McMillan/Trillian, Bill Nighy as Slartibartfast, Warwick Davis as Marvin the Paranoid Android (voiced by Alan Rickman), Anna Chancellor as Questular Rontok, John Malkovich as Humma Kavula and Kelly Macdonald as Jin Jenz Reporter.

Other cast members also included Jason Schwartzman (uncredited) as Gag Halfrunt, Edgar Wright (uncredited) as Deep Thought Tech and Simon Jones (cameo) as Magrathea Video Recording with the voices of Stephen Fry as Narrator/The Guide, Helen Mirren as Deep Thought, Richard Griffiths as Jeltz, Thomas Lennon as Eddie the Computer, Bill Bailey as The Whale, Mak Wilson as Vogon Interpreter and Garth Jennings (uncredited) as Frankie Mouse.

Producer and long-term Douglas Adams collaborator Robbie Stamp told Rob Blackwelder of *SPLICEDwire* about Freeman's casting in the movie: 'He's perfect, isn't he? When I saw his audition tape, the hairs on the back of my neck stood up. That was it. And I'll tell you what it was: It was the way he said [the famous line], "This must be Thursday. I never could get the hang of Thursdays." It had this freshly minted quality, as opposed to it feeling like a ka-ching Douglas line.'

He continued, 'He's been fabulous, and that's been a very big issue. In the end, it is this story about this ordinary guy who gets thrown out in the universe and discovers that things are as absurd out in the galaxy as they are on Earth. He's a character to whom things happen all the time, and that's quite hard without turning him into a light-saber-wielding hero. And I absolutely think we've done it. He is a man in his slippers and his dressing gown, and he's looking for a cup of tea, and he's pretty befuddled about what he's seeing out there. Douglas was working hard on the whole through-story for the film, working on Arthur's relationship with Trillian [a romantic departure from 'Hitchhiker's' previous incarnations], which I know is something that has some of the fanboys slightly exorcised.'

Sadly, author Douglas, who co-wrote the screenplay, died before production commenced in 2001. He had been trying to get a big-screen adaptation of his creation for decades but to no avail. Adams even moved to the States to get closer to Hollywood executives. It had been stuck in what is referred to as 'development hell' for the best part of twenty-six years. It was certainly his tenacity that finally got the film the green light. It's such a shame he never saw the outcome. The film is dedicated to him.

There was pressure for the creative team to make the production as faithful to the book as possible but Freeman did not let the overzealousness of the fans cause him any stress or sleepless nights. Martin knew that the film wasn't specifically made to honour the hardcore fans because the book is more of a cult classic with little mainstream attraction so, in essence, the end product had to appeal to mass audiences while also pleasing the fans. There had to be some concessions made though.

'I don't particularly go on the Internet, and I don't particularly go to Forbidden Planet and check out the vibe of the sci-fi world, because that's not the life that I live,' he told *LatinoReview*. 'But I was aware that there was something there that they'd obviously want it to be done well. I knew that was something that fans obviously cared about and cared about passionately, but we can only do what we can do, the best and the most honest interpretation of the story that we can do.'

He told AP Radio, 'We would've failed, I think, if we only made a film that was dependent on having read the book or listened to the radio series. That would've been a failure on our part because our job is to make one and three-quarter hours of entertainment... for people who know nothing about it.'

On release, *The Hitchhikers Guide to the Galaxy* was a reasonable box-office success but garnered mixed reviews from critics. It had a strong start in the US with a $21.2 million opening debut but tailed off in latter weeks. It peaked at

Number One at the US box office, ahead of the Ice Cube action thriller *XXX: State of the Union*.

Asked by Cindy Pearlman of the *Chicago Sun-Times* if it is important for an actor to have a hit movie in the States, Freeman responded, 'There are two schools of thought. Some think if you haven't made it in America, then you're a bum. Some think, "What do they know over there?" I just care that I've made a good film because in a few days, I'll either be a prick or a hero to fans of the work. I'll either be a star or it will be "Martin who?" But in the end ultimately you have to sleep with yourself and be proud on your deathbed.'

Some commented that the film tries too hard to be too British, which alienated audiences around the world, notably in the US.

'There's a long standing tradition that America takes something, doesn't quite understand it and changes it into something they do understand,' Freeman explained to *Movie Web*'s Julian Roman. 'I'm happy to report that from my experience here, that doesn't apply. I would defy anyone to see it and think that not everyone has been cast right.'

During the making of the film, M.J. Simpson, the author of the Douglas Adams biography *Hitchhiker* and former Deputy Editor of *SFX* magazine, gave the film a scathing online review, to which Freeman responded in an interview with the BBC's Alana Lee, 'You know, fair play to M.J Simpson. I couldn't say he doesn't have a right to the opinion, of course he does. And I've met him. He's a nice guy. But, ultimately, he's also a grown man who wears a Darth Vader tie. Norman Mailer he ain't.'

Freeman didn't pay too much attention to the fan scrutiny

but he was more than well aware that many fans are often disappointed by big-screen adaptations. He knew the creative team had come up with a script that was faithful to the book but he also acknowledged that the finished film wasn't going to please every single fan.

Some fans were dubious about the film version, thinking that Adams's humour would not translate too well and that the story is best left to literature; other fans were excited about the big-screen adventure. The overall opinion after the film's release was a split down the middle. In hindsight, perhaps the consensus was not so positive but the film has slowly become accepted by a larger audience of Adams fans.

'For some people this is going to be like sacrilege if it's perceived to have got it wrong,' said Freeman to the *Washington Post*'s Alona Wartofsky. 'But I couldn't go to work with that feeling, and I couldn't really go and do my job if I was paying too much mind to that. I just... tried to play him in the best way I could.'

Freeman and the rest of the cast and crew received very positive feedback from Adams's family – his widow and son. They hadn't made a perfect film by any means, as the critical response can attest, but they were respectful to the script Adams had left. Freeman even caught up with Adams's family at the film's premiere and they were delighted with the outcome.

So what did the critics think of the finished product?

Writing in *The Guardian*, Peter Bradshaw said, 'Martin Freeman (Tim from *The Office*) is inspired casting as Dent, and delivers exactly the right note of futile English sarcasm in the face of complete and utter planetary destruction. His best friend, the oddly named Ford Prefect, tips him off about what is about to happen; together they escape and hitch-hike across the Milky Way, armed with their invaluable book, the *Hitchhiker's Guide*, voiced with lucid serenity by Stephen Fry.'

Darren Waters wrote on *BBC Movies*, 'Despite outstanding production design and some fantastic visual effects, overall the film is a bit of a mess. A charming mess, maybe, but a mess all the same. Did the script veer too far away from the source material or tie itself in knots trying to keep faith with it? Bizarrely, I think the answer is both.'

Peter Travers was more enthusiastic in his three out of five-star *Rolling Stone* review: 'The mission impossible, which first-time director Garth Jennings has bravely accepted, is to hold true to the droll, aggressive, very British verbal humour of the creator Douglas Adams (he died in 2001) in a movie that spills over with visual gags, puppet monsters and a digital John Malkovich ... the script by Karey Kirkpatrick and Adams himself delivers the goods in inspired lunacy.'

Hilariously, the DVD release features scenes that were filmed but were never actually meant for the movie.

'We did, yeah,' admitted Freeman to *Empire* magazine when asked about the scenes that were not included. 'It was a nod towards the people who thought it was going to be ruined because it was American. So we just shot some ridiculously Hollywood-y, horrible, over-the-top, clichéd, action-movie style portrayals ... but Garth's idea was "Let's just have some fun and pretend that these were the ones we edited out." That was good fun.'

A sequel, *The Restaurant at the End of the Universe*, was originally planned but Martin Freeman confirmed to MTV

Movie Blog in 2007 that a sequel was unlikely to happen, saying, 'I found that out from the horse's mouth, [director] Garth Jennings. I had dinner with him and he said [the first one] just didn't do well enough.'

There was a little bit of room for improvisation but not a great deal and it was unnecessary, anyway, because it was Adams's story, dialogue and humour that made the film what it was. The creative team were careful not to dilute the film with their own ideas. Freeman wasn't interested in starring in films with special effects and action scenes, which is ironic considering the trilogy of films he would later be known for, so *The Hitchhiker's Guide to the Galaxy* did not change his career path but rather his bank balance. He got into acting to star in films like *Twelve Angry Men* – serious, realistic dramas.

Perhaps playing Arthur Dent did not do much to dissuade people from naturally assuming Freeman to be an everyday bloke. After all, Tim Canterbury and Arthur Dent are, in their own ways, normal guys. He was pigeonholed as an actor and it would be quite some time before that would change.

'Compared to a lot of people, I'm a big-mouth show-off, d'you know what I mean?' Martin admitted to the *Globe And Mail*'s Simon Houpt. 'But in show-biz terms I don't think I am, because I don't go to every event and I don't particularly want people to know everything about my life, and I don't live my life through that medium. I could be on the telly all the time and I could be everywhere all the time and I certainly don't want to be, because I do think only a… moron wants that, or someone with a bigger hole in their lives than I ever would want to have.'

With two major films under his belt in *Love Actually* and

The Hitchhiker's Guide to the Galaxy, one might now think that Freeman was interested in achieving success on the other side of the Atlantic. Not so. He didn't even have an American agent, preferring to stick with his London one.

'I'm not interested in living that life,' Freeman confessed to the *London Evening Standard*'s Bruce Dessau in 2005. 'I've never wanted to go to lovely LA. I was a well-respected actor before *The Office* and there's lots of other work I've been proud of that is less well known. I consider myself primarily a stage actor and if people were only giving me work now because of Tim I'd feel a bit of a fraud. It's funny because until I became the nicest man in Britain I tended to be cast as villains, drug dealers, rent boys and bare-knuckle fighters.'

Further TV work continued as he was cast in the comedy TV film *Not Tonight with John Sergeant*, which was broadcast on 22 May 2005.

Freeman admitted to Bruce Dessau of the *London Evening Standard* in 2004 that he is tired of seeing comedians who think they are actors. 'It's hard enough for actors anyway,' he said. 'There's a roller coaster of dreadful casting that no one has the guts to stop. There's nothing more painful than seeing comics who can't act – it makes me want to set fire to people's fucking houses.'

Martin's choice of roles tended to be very safe; almost middle-of-the-road. He admitted that sometimes it is better not to know why actors get cast in certain roles, as he explained to Tom Cardy of New Zealand's *Stuff*: 'I think, sometimes you gotta be careful what you wish for. Of course we all want to be told we're brilliant for various ways, however we hope we're brilliant. And then, if someone thinks we're brilliant for a reason we find unflattering, then we'd rather not hear it. 'Cause of course there's a difference, like with any actor, between the parts that I play, and... For a start, no one's seen everything I've done, apart from me. And I've played a lot of parts over seventeen years.

'There's a difference between the parts that I play, and who I am, and who people think I am,' he added. 'There's quite a big discrepancy sometimes, between those things.'

Freeman was then cast in the role of Ed Robinson in the six-episode 2005 series of *The Robinsons*, which began airing in May. The series was written and directed by Mark Bussell and Justin Sbresni, with executive producers that included Jon Plowman and Michele Buck.

'It didn't feel like a return to telly to me because I'd always done lots of TV and I just follow whatever script is good at the time,' he told *Dark Horizon*'s Paul Fischer. 'An awful lot of film scripts are dreadful while a lot of telly scripts are really good. So I just want to be involved in things that I like. I'm as proud of *The Robinsons* as anything else I've done. I mean I love it. But again, whether anyone else loves it, I hope they do.'

The Robinsons is a British comedy about lead character Ed Robinson's (Freeman) relationship with his family, including his parents (played by Anna Massey and Richard Johnson), who are constantly nagging at each other, his successful older brother George (Hugh Bonneville) and his sister Vicky (Abigail Cruttenden), who has to have everything perfect. Ed is a divorced reinsurance actuary but gets fired and moves in with his aunt. He begins to rethink his life and looks to find a career that he has a passion for and a steady girlfriend.

Kathryn Flett wrote in *The Observer*, 'Freeman gets the star billing and the cute voice-overs but despite being enormously likeable – to the point where, if our paths ever cross, I will have to restrain myself from pinching his cheeks, ruffling his hair and pulling the sort of face I normally reserve for winsome toddlers – Freeman is almost outshone by an awesomely fine supporting cast.'

But back to Hitchikers, the bigger the film, the more expansive the marketing campaign. As it was Freeman's first Hollywood movie, he had a great deal of promotional work to fulfil in the wake of the film's release.

Martin has always found the whirlwind press junkets a laborious but obligatory task; a necessary evil of the job, 'answering the same questions over and over again. With some exceptions, and with the best will in the world, you do get tired. Obviously you just have to pinch yourself,' he told reporters, including *Dark Horizon*'s Paul Fischer, at a junket for *The Hitchhiker's Guide to the Galaxy*, 'you have to make it interesting for yourself, hopefully make it interesting for the press, but also to a certain extent, that's only part of the job.'

Freeman continued to dip his toes into the odd left-field venture. He played 'The Man' in *Round About Five*, a long-forgotten short film that was released on 22 August 2005. Freeman's character is desperate to get across London to meet his girlfriend (Lena Headey) off the Eurostar and pursues an attractive bicycle courier (Jodhi May) to take him on the back of her bike, which ultimately creates a romantic predicament for him.

The actor had been in many TV and film productions but

he struggled to find the time to explore his thespian talents in the theatre, so it was a delight when he was offered a chance to star in a London theatre production. Freeman committed to a three-and-a-half-week run of *Blue Eyes and Heels* (written by Toby Whithouse) at Soho Theatre in October 2005.

'Career-wise,' Freeman admitted to the *London Evening Standard*'s Bruce Dessau at the time, 'this is not what I should be doing, but I really like the play and there aren't many things that I really like. I wanted to avoid anything that was too commercial. It's not that I want to be poor, it's just that I don't want money to be the main thing.'

The play follows Duncan (Freeman), an ambitious young TV producer looking for his next hit to secure a career at an independent TV-production company. He plans to bring wrestling back to TV screens and meets Victor (John McNeill), an actor best known for his role as the Count of Monte Cristo. Past his best and looking to reclaim his prime, Victor is perfect fodder for Duncan's plan to climb the media-industry ladder and secure a promotion. Along the way, Duncan meets a career-obsessive PA played by Sandra Eldridge. However, they clash, as Duncan believes in the trash he is peddling, while the PA believes in quality. Such are the times, where trash sells and quality sinks. *Blues Eyes and Heels* attempts to be a satire on modern times of trashy tabloid TV.

Theatre pundit Michael Billington was critical of the play in his two out of five-star review in *The Guardian* but he praised Freeman: 'The real pleasure lies in watching Martin Freeman, late of *The Office*, who reminds us what a brilliant comic actor he is. His Duncan is a bundle of staccato gestures and panic-stricken smiles, confirming that TV companies thrive on a hierarchy of insecurity. And his vain attempt to leap athletically into the wrestling ring is worthy of Woody Allen.'

John Thaxter of the *British Theatre Guide* wrote, 'Toby Whithouse's superbly written three-hander reminded me strongly of Brian Friel's Faith Healer, sustained dialogue replacing Friel's extended solo pieces but with equal impact, both comic and sad. It could make a brilliant one-off play for television, except that in a multichannel world we no longer enjoy the luxury of one-off plays.'

Stage Noise's Gabby Bermingham enthused, 'The play provides valid and insightful commentary on what I assume is modern media morality. One feature I particularly loved was the development of Duncan's character. On the one hand he is supercilious, insincere and heartless. Hand in hand with these undesirable qualities is the fact that he is also a true believer. He is the voice of popular culture, he believes his own spin, and the value of what he 'creates'. I also could not let this go without noting that Whithouse chooses the female character to give voice to the arguments for taste, intelligence and ethics.'

Freeman also took part in a Marks & Spencer celebrity ad campaign, which was shot by renowned photographer David Bailey. At this point Martin's intolerance for things earned him the nickname 'Uncle Joe' among his friends. It is a reference to Stalin. Freeman was doing rather well for himself by this point and things would only get bigger and better.

Martin admitted to *Empire* in 2005, 'I'm not exactly a well-seasoned, great screen actor, you know. I'm still learning the ropes, but as far as I see it my job doesn't change that much. You certainly don't act bigger. If anything, you act smaller because the screen is going to be so much bigger. It's very easy to look like you're overdoing it on a big screen, you know, because the raising of an eyebrow says so much more than it would do on a television screen.'

Freeman and his wife had their first child, Joe, in 2006. Despite Martin's brief venture into Hollywood and his success in *The Office*, the actor was still searching for that all-elusive break. With a wife and a newborn baby, he needed a steady pay cheque and regular work to tend to his family on a financial level.

As previously mentioned, Freeman is a connoisseur of classic R&B and soul music and has an extensive record collection in his home. He hosted a semi-regular 2006 BBC Radio 2 show called *The Great Unknown*, which aired in six episodes over October and November and saw each instalment focus on a different recording artist. He began with the Staple Singers and moved on to Boz Scaggs, Ramsey Lewis, Traffic, Roberta Flack and The Band.

He'd been making mix tapes all his life – mostly on cassette – but had recently moved on to CDs. Making a mix tape was one of the first things he always did for a woman prior to meeting his lifelong partner. He would use it as a sort of a test to see how a woman would respond to the music and to judge whether they'd get on well with each other. He said he found that women can be more direct than men – they'll simply say whether they like it or not but men can be snobbish about music.

'If I'm making a tape for Amanda, my other half, she won't

be impressed if I've got an original pressing of a song, or some B-side that's been out of print for years,' he said to *Tiny Mix Tapes* in 2007. 'When I pick songs for her, all I think about is, "She'd really like this and it'll make her happy."'

As soon as he'd met Abbington, he'd stopped making mix tapes for his friends because it is such a personal thing to do. He usually centred the songs around a theme, which made it even more personal. He always waited with apprehensive eagerness to see to how his partner/friend would respond to the songs.

His main passion is vinyl as he prefers the feel and look of a record over a CD. He appreciates the cover artwork, which he feels looks more impressive on the cover of a vinyl record. As with many music aficionados, Freeman doesn't feel as though he owns a piece of music until he has the vinyl copy. There are CDs and iPods in his house but the process of putting the needle down on the record and sitting in a room surrounded by thousands of records is a ritual that he enjoys greatly.

'And that's especially true for me, because 70 per cent of the music I enjoy came out originally on analog,' he explained to *Tiny Mix Tapes*. 'If you get a good copy, that's how it should be heard. Obviously, if you're listening to a really scratchy record, then of course a CD will sound better. But it'll never compare with a pressing on vinyl. As I've gotten older and have a bit more money, I can afford to be more anal about that kinda stuff. I know I'm entering into mental territory, but I like it. I like thinking, "Well, I've got that record already, but I only have the reissue, and it's not great and I'd like to find the original."'

Freeman prefers going into record shops to look for music rather than using online stores such as eBay. He was ecstatic to find a rare Syreeta 7-inch called 'To Know You Is To Love You', which was co-written and produced by Stevie Wonder, for £2.50 at a record shop in Yorkshire, where he was doing some theatre work.

One of his favourite stores is Retrobloke.com in Hendon, North London, where he has bought all sorts of soul and jazz records, including releases by Tina Turner, Don Ellis and Gladys Knight & The Pips.

Freeman even released a compilation in 2006 of his favourite obscure soul music called *Martin Freeman Presents... Made to Measure*. His photo is on the CD cover. He thought that people would recognise him off the telly, be intrigued enough to buy the CD and have their minds opened up to a whole new world of music that they may not have been familiar with. His aim was noble.

'... it was an amazing honour,' he expressed to the *Metro*'s Andrew Williams. 'Soul music is the cornerstone of what I listen to. I just had to put twenty of my favourite motown songs together. I wanted a mixture of things people knew and also didn't know.'

The collection consists of 'I Want You Back' (Jackson 5, The Corporation TM), 'No Matter What Sign You Are (Berry Gordy Jr., Diana Ross & The Supremes, Henry Cosby), 'You've Made Me So Very Happy' (Berry Gordy Jr., Brenda Holloway), 'The Night' (Frankie Valli and The Four Seasons), 'Ooo Baby Baby' (Smokey Robinson & The Miracles), 'The Bells' (Marvin Gaye, The Originals), 'Please Don't Stay (Once You Go Away)' (Art Stewart, Cal Harris, Ed Townsend, Marvin Gaye), 'Ball Of Confusion (That's What The World Is Today)' (Norman

Whitfield, The Temptations), 'I Feel Sanctified' (Commodores, James Anthony Carmichael, Jeffrey Bowen), 'Sugar' (Stevie Wonder), 'The Hunter Gets Captured By The Game' (Smokey Robinson, The Marvelettes), 'From Head To Toe' (Chris Clark, Smokey Robinson), 'Never Can Say Goodbye' (Hal Davis, Jackson 5, Gene Page), 'Trouble Man' (Marvin Gaye), 'Still Water (Love)' (Four Tops, Frank Wilson, Jimmy Roach, Jerry Long), 'It's A Shame' (Stevie Wonder, The Spinners), 'Bad Weather' (Stevie Wonder, The Supremes), 'Stop Her On Sight (S.O.S.)' (Al Kent, Edwin Starr, Richard Morris), 'The Tears Of A Clown' (Smokey Robinson & The Miracles, Henry Cosby) and 'To Know You Is To Love You' (Stevie Wonder, Syreeta).

Aside from Freeman's forays into the musical world, on the acting front, 2006 was a busy year.

From 25–30 April Martin was one of the guest stars in *The Exonerated*, the hit drama about life on death row, which ran at West London's Riverside Studios until 11 June 2006. Guest stars during its sixteen-week run included Stockard Channing, Kristin Davis, Danny Glover, Catherine Tate, Aidan Quinn, Richard Dreyfuss, Kate Mulgrew, Peri Gilpin, Martin Freeman, Mike McShane, Henry Goodman, Mackenzie Crook and Vanessa Redgrave.

The play was written in 2001 by creative husband-and-wife duo Jessica Blank and Erik Jensen. The ninety-minute play was based on interviews with forty former death-row prisoners and focused on those convicts who were wrongfully imprisoned for between two and twenty-two years. The off-Broadway run finished in October 2002 after 608 performances, with guest stars that also included Gabriel Byrne, Richard Dreyfuss, Mia

Farrow, Jeff Goldblum, Alanis Morissette, Lynn Redgrave, Ally Sheedy, Brooke Shields, Kathleen Turner and Debra Winger. It was later adapted for TV and starred Hollywood actors Brian Dennehy, Danny Glover, Susan Sarandon and Aidan Quinn, who also appeared in the Edinburgh production.

2006 saw the release of two films starring Freeman: he played Matt in *Confetti* and Sandy in *Breaking and Entering*.

Confetti, released on 5 May, is a British romantic comedy filmed in a fly-on-the-wall-style-documentary fashion, similar to that of *The Office*. It is about a bridal-magazine competition for the most original wedding. Three couples are chosen to compete for the ultimate prize of a house. The script was completely improvised and the film stars Jessica Stevenson, Jimmy Carr, Mark Heap, Julia Davis, Robert Webb, and Olivia Colman. Improvising the comedy with the characters and furthering the story was a handful and difficult to juggle all at once. It took a great deal of effort for all concerned.

On the subject of improvisation, Freeman explained to *Empire*, 'I'm very happy when there's a rough script or a rough thing saying where a scene should go and you've got to find your own way there. But when we've not even decided on where a scene's going to go, that's quite scary. I think we all thought, "I'll be able to do this," but you kind of forget there's a difference between being a bit rock 'n' roll with the dialogue and absolutely making it all up.'

Improvisation has to be real, dramatic and funny, so it was a challenging endeavour for everyone. They all knew how the scene would start but not how it would end.

'At times I felt that I wasn't very good at it,' he elaborated to Siobhan Synnot of *Douban*, 'but it helped that the film was shot as a documentary, so it was okay for people to stumble over their words and talk over each other, because that's what happens in real life.' Not knowing what the other characters might say next kept him on his toes – but sometimes the gags brought shooting to a standstill as Martin and co-stars cracked up. 'There's one scene that didn't make the film because I'm struggling to try on a pair of wedding shoes and Jason Watkins, who plays a very camp wedding planner, comes up behind me and says, "Here, let me give you the horn." I had to turn away from the camera because I was laughing so much.'

Empire's Angie Errigo wrote, 'Most believable are couple number one, Matt and Sam (Martin Freeman and Jessica Stevenson). These two are sweeties who love musicals and want to play Fred Astaire and Ginger Rogers on their big day – if they can nudge mother-of-the-bride Steadman and Sam's pushy cruise-entertainer sister out of the spotlight for once.'

Total Film magazine said, 'Largely improvised, *Confetti* relies heavily on the considerable talents of its Brit TV stars, whose inventiveness make for a beguiling mixture of moving moments, sniggers and excruciating silences.'

Directed by the late Anthony Minghella and starring lead actors Jude Law, Juliette Binoche and Robin Wright Penn, *Breaking and Entering* is a romantic crime drama set in an inner-city neighbourhood of London about a successful landscape architect who comes into contact with a young thief and his mother, which causes him to re-evaluate his life. Released on 10 November, the film received negative reviews from critics and was not a box-office success.

The Guardian's Peter Bradshaw wrote of the production, 'But the film is full of interesting characters, intelligently conceived scenes and funny lines – particularly from Martin Freeman as Law's long-suffering partner in the architectural practice. Juliet Stevenson plays Law's therapist, a role that recalls her famous therapy scene in Minghella's 1991 film *Truly, Madly, Deeply*.'

Exclaim.ca's Travis Mackenzie Hoover said, 'True, Vera Farmiga and *The Office*'s Martin Freeman shine as a prostitute and Law's second-in-command, respectively; they manage to evoke inner life and nuance beyond what their sketchy roles suggest. But in the end, the movie is cheesy liberal self-congratulation masquerading as social conscience, and it won't satisfy anyone who's looking for something substantial.'

As the months rolled by, Martin Freeman stacked up yet more credentials to his name but, in truth, these acting challenges were of little substance. He needed more meat-and-potatoes roles; parts that would define his career and shape his future thespian endeavours.

Long Hot Summer was shown in late 2006, and was about three friends who decide to share a house together in London over the summer, but tensions mount as truths are revealed and their friendship is put to the test. The film was written and directed by Matt Hilliard-Forde and also stars Michael Alexander, Lucy Briers, Jessica Brohn and Simon Cox.

Preceded by *Shaun of the Dead*, *Hot Fuzz* is the second in the *Three Flavors Cornetto Trilogy*. Inspired by such action films as *Lethal Weapon*, *Point Break* and *Executive Decision*, *Hot Fuzz* is a comedy police procedural. Simon Pegg and Nick Frost play two officers trying to solve a series of mysterious deaths in a small English village. It was filmed over an eleven-week period in early 2006. Freeman joins an ensemble cast of actors who make minor appearances: Bill Bailey, Steve Coogan and Bill Nighy crop up, as do villagers played by Kenneth Cranham, Maria Charles, Peter Wight, Julia Deakin, Patricia Franklin, Lorraine Hilton and Tim Barlow, and there are cameos by Stephen Merchant as Peter Ian Staker, Cate Blanchett as Janine, director Peter Jackson as Father Christmas and, finally, Garth Jennings as a drug dealer.

Hot Fuzz was a commercial and critical success after it opened on 14 February in cinemas in the UK and on 20 April in the US. Olly Richards of *Empireonline.com* wrote, '*Fuzz* never quite achieves the boundless creativity of *Shaun*, but Wright and Pegg throw every joke they have at the concept until they tickle the audience into giddy submission.'

Despite his growing reputation and a curious CV that was the envy of his peers, did his connection to *The Office* weigh on him like the proverbial albatross? After all, he was seemingly trying so hard to move away from its everlasting shadow.

'No, I'm not sick of talking about *The Office*,' Freeman said to *TV Guide*'s Ethan Alter. 'I really do understand people's fascination with it. To do one of the most-talked-about shows in the last few years this early on in my career... that opportunity doesn't come along very often. It's definitely a thing to beat.'

Freeman, however, was finally coming round to the idea that America would offer more opportunities and that he could balance projects on both sides of the Atlantic.

CHAPTER FIVE

AMERICAN FILMS, BRITISH ACTOR

'People thought, "Danny Dyer and Martin Freeman in a film
together? That sounds good," but actually they hated it.'
FREEMAN SPEAKING TO CHRIS SULLIVAN,
DAILY MAIL, 2008

Though he may have only had a minor role in *Hot Fuzz*, Martin Freeman was gaining enough credible roles and minor parts in successful movies that his name and face were becoming more prominent in Britain and elsewhere. He was still best known as Tim Canterbury in *The Office* and he was not yet the household name he would one day become but, as jobbing actors go, he was becoming rather successful.

Dedication, released in August 2007, is an American romantic comedy about Henry Roth (Billy Crudup), who is an obsessive compulsive and a children's-book writer. His illustrator and sole friend, Rudy (Tom Wilkinson), dies after a successful collaboration on their children's-books series *Marty The Beaver*. Henry has to produce another book in the series in time for Christmas and is under pressure from his publisher, Arthur Planck (Bob Balaban). An illustrator named Lucy Reilly (Mandy Moore) is assigned to work with Henry. However, her ex-boyfriend (Freeman) is back on the scene and attempts to wow her back after having dedicated his latest book to her. *Dedication* was not a box-office success nor did it win over the critics.

Jeannette Catsoulis of *The New York Times* wrote, 'The directing debut of the actor Justin Theroux, *Dedication* is almost saved by David Bromberg's tart dialogue and exceptional acting from its three leads.'

Jesse Hassenger of *Contact Music.com* wrote, 'Though the script may be the culprit for the mismatched clichés and broad supporting characters (chief among them Dianne Weist as Moore's shrieking mother), it's disappointing that Theroux wasn't able to finesse it into something more nuanced and clear.'

The Good Night is an American romantic comedy starring Gwyneth Paltrow, Penélope Cruz, Martin Freeman, Danny DeVito and Simon Pegg and is set between London and New York. Freeman plays Gary Shaller, a former pop star who now makes a living writing jingles for commercials and experiences a midlife crisis. Freeman may not have been able to relate to his character on a deeply personal level, even though there have been times when Martin has had similar crises of confidence, as experienced by many, but all it takes is imagination and empathy to understand Gary. He's a failed musician who is frustrated with life. It's a universal theme.

Gary tries to live out his dreams and Freeman is a person who's had some indelible, recurring dreams, as he told *IGN. com*'s Leigh Singer: 'I've had several really tangible dreams about UFOs and they've been amazing! You know that sort of everyday quality that you get in a couple of scenes in *Close Encounters* [*of the Third Kind*] where these lights fly over a road and it somehow seems tangible, somehow seems real. I've had a few of those dreams about UFOs where it's been absolutely clear that this is the day that the world changes and it's very exciting. I've not had one of those for a while, but I love them when I have them!'

It was director Jake Paltrow's first feature and, as such, he didn't want his famous sister overshadowing him too much, so she was not involved initially. As time progressed, however, he reasoned that he'd got an outstanding actor for a sister who knows the material and was volunteering her talents, most likely for a fee cut, given the nature of the film's budget.

'Jake Paltrow contacted me while I was making *The Hitchhiker's Guide to the Galaxy* three years ago and sent me the script,' Freeman explained to *NYC Movie Guru*. 'I responded to it very positively. It was original and I thought it had a true voice. I like working with people who just like to tell a story. [Jake Paltrow] adores film, so it was a joy to work with somebody with that passion.'

He added, 'The ending is one of the reasons I wanted to do it. When I got to the last page [of the script], I thought it was a great way to finish it – sort of, unresolved. It could have been a lot happier. I like knowing that it's enough for him to keep dreaming.'

From the get-go Freeman got along with the writer/director Jake, who had also directed episodes of the acclaimed cop series *NYPD Blue*. Their initial phone conversation lasted almost an hour and they shared similar ideas for what the tone of the film should be. If Paltrow did not write the role specifically for

Freeman, he was certainly one of the director's top choices of actors for the part. They were both working on faith; Martin hadn't seen anything Paltrow had been involved with, while the director had only seen a couple of things Freeman had starred in. Life is too short, Freeman thought, so he committed to the script. The script was Paltrow's vision and Martin could see that. It wasn't a script churned out by a committee of writers to appease a certain audience demographic but rather the sole idea of a committed film-maker.

Freeman didn't actually consider himself to be a bona-fide movie star, so he was pleased that he was approached for the part. Americans knew Freeman mostly for *The Office* and *Love Actually* at this stage in his career. Paltrow did not need convincing to cast Freeman but perhaps the rest of the cast needed to be persuaded because Martin wasn't a household name and, as such, the film had less box-office appeal. Paltrow put their minds at rest and Freeman was more than happy that someone he hardly knew – almost a stranger – saw something in him to warrant a lead role in a US movie.

'I read a lot of American scripts that are better than British scripts,' he admitted to *Movie Web.com*'s Julian Roman. 'They're for grown-ups. They're not trying to remake *The Italian Job*. We do a lot of capery stuff in Britain and a lot of American scripts are a bit more grown-up.'

Freeman didn't actually know that his female cast would be Gwyneth Paltrow and Penélope Cruz. He also got a kick out of working with his old mate Simon Pegg, whom he lobbied to be in the film. Both actors have a very truthful, honest and un-egotistical nature about them. Martin sees that there's a seriousness to Pegg, though he may be best known as a comedian because of *Spaced* and *Shaun of the Dead*. He's not begging to be liked on screen all the time. Pegg has great timing too. Some comedians are awful as serious actors, some are excellent; Pegg has a natural acting talent.

Martin enjoyed working with both Paltrows; he'd never met Gwyneth before but Simon Pegg knew her through her then husband, Coldplay singer Chris Martin. Freeman took to her straight away. She was very easy to work with and did not bring any Hollywood ego with her, which Freeman admired. She is an excellent actress and he has a great deal of respect for her because of that.

Everyone in the film was excellently suited to their role. There was a vibe, a relentless energy on set that came from the outstanding cast. Another key member of the company was Danny DeVito. During filming on the streets of New York, people were thrilled to see him; teachers, cops, everyday Joes, children and parents. Freeman found him to be immediately likeable and a delight to work with. He's a celebrity but he's approachable. DeVito is an interesting man and Martin enjoyed their scenes together.

The film is set in New York, where there is an artistic community, similar to that in London. There is great cultural life in both cities and it's a rat race to get jobs, especially for creative people. Creative people are attracted to cosmopolitan cities but it's a dog-eat-dog world. Freeman, unlike his character in the film, has never been out of work.

Martin spoke to *Ain't It Cool News* writer Capone about the film's melancholy ambience: 'I like the sort of calm of melancholy and also the stability of that. So, you sort of know where you are, which I like. Yeah, the film does have that quality, I suppose. I think it might have less of it, as you say, depending on what expectation you bring to it. Because if someone said to you, "God, it's a really, really depressing film," then you'd go, "No, no, there are really quite a lot of laughs in it." But, yeah, if you're expecting a lot of laughs, there are some laughs in it, but yeah, it's darker than that, I suppose, which is exactly… well, I suppose it partly reflects my taste in films, and in art generally, and in life.'

The Good Night was released on 5 October 2007 in the US and, finally, in the UK on 18 January 2008. It wasn't exactly a successful film on the financial front.

Cinema Blend.com's Katey Rich wrote, 'Despite its structural flaws, *The Good Night* features some fine performances – Pegg and Freeman are a joy to watch together – and characters who, while under drawn, earn our sympathy without being cloying or too self-absorbed. Paltrow may have a career as a director ahead of him, but as a screenwriter, his ideas come out muddled and, well, tired. Like someone else's "fascinating" dream, *The Good Night* never turns out as interesting as its teller thinks it is.'

Lisa Schwarzbaum of *Entertainment Weekly* wrote, 'Martin Freeman, from the BBC's *The Office*, has just the right semi-stunned mug to play a guy sliding into work-and-love loserdom who finds solace from his undermining girlfriend with a dream woman he encounters in his sleep.'

Meanwhile, his former *Office* colleague Ricky Gervais had also set his sights on Hollywood success and was doing rather well with 2006's *Night at the Museum*, 2007's *Stardust* and the soon-to-be-released *Ghost Town* in 2008. Gervais would go on to have considerable success in the US and become just as well known across the Atlantic as he is in his native Britain.

'I'm not surprised he's done well,' Freeman expressed to Andrew Duncan of *Reader's Digest*. 'They like gall and what they perceive as British cheek, straight talking, irony and sarcasm. He's always sailed pretty close to the wind, so good for him. I dreamed of a Hollywood career as an eighteen-year-old sitting in the bath, but dreams and reality are very different.'

Freeman and Abbington were a happy couple living the married life, although they are not actually married. Martin is somewhat dubious about the concept of marriage, believing that it's more like a business arrangement than an act of love. He's known people who are together for years but split up after getting married.

'I've not been to many weddings but not that long ago I was asked to do a reading at a wedding and I couldn't do it. It was really embarrassing,' he admitted in 2012 to *Douban. com* journalist Siobhan Synnot. 'It was impossible for me to get through without breaking down. It took me about twenty minutes to do and in the end one of my brothers had to get up and put his arm around my shoulder for moral support before I could do it. I'm sure everyone thought I was just another luvvie, auditioning for a role.'

Both Freeman's and his Abbington's respective careers were flourishing and they have always supported each other's work, although the latter has admitted she does get the odd wave of insecurity and it was during the making of *The Good Night*, where Freeman was cast opposite two gorgeous Hollywood women, that she got a tad jealous.

'I was eight-and-a-half months' pregnant and bigger than a house,' Abbington confessed to the *Daily Mail*'s Vicky Power. 'And Penelope's so beautiful and talented, who wouldn't fancy her?'

Even though Freeman's fame has far eclipsed Abbington's, he has not developed an ego, nor allowed others to treat her poorly.

'But he always says, "And this is my girlfriend,"' Abbington said to the *Mail*'s Vicki Power. 'Only recently some girl came up to him and shoved me out of the way. And he said "Excuse me, this is my girlfriend, don't push her out of the way."'

Martin Freeman had become an unlikely sex symbol along with such fellow actors as Brit Simon Pegg and American Seth Rogen.

He spoke to *Nerve.com*'s Alexis Tirado and described how he felt about this: 'As soon as you're branded anything, that's not great. It's just another lazy way of marketing people. If you look out your window, most people in the world don't look like Brad Pitt, but they all have wives. The whole idea of, "Paul Giamatti is kind of sexy." Well, yeah he's sexy. Ask his fucking wife or anyone he's ever laid.'

He continued, 'Is it surprising? No, because attraction doesn't come from abs and pecs. It comes from somewhere else altogether. If Penélope Cruz was a shit actress, no one would fancy her. It's that simple. Because the actresses who are beautiful and act like shit are going to be forgotten in about five days. So it's a double-edged sword, because people are like,

"Hey, you're sexy! But you're kind of ugly!" I'm not supposed to be happy about that.'

Freeman later starred in the Gavin Claxton written and directed film *The All Together*, released on 11 May 2007. It is a British comedy film starring Martin in the lead role as a hacked-off TV producer and aspiring screenwriter named Chris, who has a distaste for British gangster films. He leaves his flatmate Bob (Velibor Topic) in charge of showing estate agents around the house that he is trying to sell. Chris is concerned that Bob will spend all day in the basement playing loud music and miss the estate agent's call but Chris asks him to listen out for the doorbell anyway and show anyone around who visits. Bob promises Chris he will do that. While the screenwriter struggles with a day at work, Bob takes his instructions rather too literally and allows anyone who comes calling inside the house to look around. That includes a young British fella (played by Danny Dyer) and an American (played by Corey Johnston). When Chris returns home that evening, he finds his flatmate, four estate agents, two Jehovah's Witnesses and a children's entertainer held hostage by the Brit and American: two archetypal gangsters that could be straight out of a British gangster film. It's hardly taxing stuff and many of the jokes fall flat but it was good to see Freeman in a lead role, even if it was with Danny Dyer, an actor whose pedigree of films is hardly thought of as high quality.

It was Freeman's partner and fellow actor, Amanda Abbington, who suggested that Martin should go for the role. When she got back home after her own audition, Freeman asked her how it went and she said it went well and that there's a role in the film that would be perfect for him so he should go for it. He took a look at the script, liked it and met with the director and subsequently got the part. There was a point to the film and Freeman didn't feel as though it was written to particularly win over American audiences. There was a heart to the movie and an honesty that Martin admired. It wasn't written with the idea of making box-office millions. Generally, Freeman enjoys home-grown products. However, there is far more opportunity for success in America, with a much wider choice of roles available to an aspiring actor.

It was a frantic eighteen-day shoot but Freeman enjoyed working with the cast and crew, especially the director. There was determination and courage in everyone. They strove to make as good a film as they possibly could. He was under no illusion that it would make him rich, but he also thought the script was truthfully written.

Speaking about the very busy set, he told Rob Carnevale of *Indie London.co.uk*, 'I was quite ill for some of my shoot because I had a real stinking cold. There's no denying it was a hard shoot – not hard like being in Bosnia hard! – but it was hard by the standards of making a film. But that hardship engendered something else that was quite fun too – that Dunkirk spirit and a feeling of, "We've just got to do this".'

No one in the film was of any high status, there were no major egos and the upside of having little budget and a taut shooting deadline was that there was camaraderie, a similar spirit amongst a cast as when working in the theatre or even on radio. No one had their own space so they had to get long. There was no other option but to get to know each other.

On working with his real life partner, Freeman said to BBC Movies' Rob Carnevale, 'We've done it before a few times and I do always really enjoy it. She's a brilliant actress and I respect what she does. Obviously I love her too. So it's easy. There's no other politics like I'm doing the scene with someone I don't really like. Anything we don't like about each other we can say [laughs].'

Released in May, *The All Together*, has been long forgotten about. There are, potentially, many roles that Freeman might care to forget but such is the life of a now successful and revered actor who once took as many parts as possibly in order to make a living, as is the case with any jobbing actor in an increasingly fickle industry.

Martin believes a gangster thriller is better suited to his thespian skills than, say, an action film. 'I can't see that people would ever ask me to do it,' he admitted to *Nerve.com*'s Alexis Tirado. 'I'm not famous enough. I'm not box-office enough. I can run and I'm fit, but there are some people better suited to that. Also, I don't want to play the guy in the yacht with no problems. That's certainly not a reflection of my life. As a person, I'm not smooth, do you know what I mean? I can't do smooth very easily.'

The Guardian's Phelim O'Neill wrote, 'Nothing about the situation nor the characters rings even slightly true, and no laughs ever come from the increasingly desperate attempts to shoe-horn gags in. Freeman seems to have been given no direction other than "be like that guy from *The Office*". Utterly pointless.'

Jack Foley of *IndieLondon.co.uk* said, 'Only Freeman emerges with any credit, somehow managing to remain endearing in spite of the contrived nature of his own storyline (the brief scenes he shares with real-life girlfriend Amanda Abbington offer brief respite from an otherwise rotten experience).'

He continued, 'Even a clever cine-literate monologue from Freeman that begins the movie is ruthlessly exposed as pretentious come the implausible finale. *The All Together* therefore carries with it the wretched stench of yet another disappointing farce for the British industry...'

Time Out's David Jenkins wrote, 'As misanthropic TV producer Charlie, Martin Freeman reassumes all the tics that won him an army of fans in *The Office* while Danny Dyer pops up playing, well, Danny Dyer, confirming that he wouldn't know a good script if it struck him over the head with a pool cue. The few laughs come care of Velibor Topic as wacky Bosnian housemate Bob, who harbours a penchant for combining taxidermy and pornography (you do the math).'

Freeman also appeared in two short British films in 2007. He was the voice of 'The Pig' in one of them, called *Lonely Hearts*. Written and directed by James Keaton, *Lonely Hearts* is set one year after Jeff's (Ralph Haddon) wife leaves him and attempts to get over it by meeting women by way of 'lonely-hearts' dating. Jeff struggles to move on until he starts talking to a soft-toy pig that gives him advice on dating. Jeff meets an attractive woman in a sandwich shop and remembers that he promised to take the pig along with him on his next date.

In *Rubbish*, released in June 2007, he starred alongside Anna Friel and James Lance. The film's estimated budget was £20,000, and it sees Freeman taking out the rubbish one morning, spotting a local woman and trying to impress her.

Martin was next seen in the Bill Kenwright theatre production of *The Last Laugh*. Before a highly publicised move to the West End, the production opened at the Theatre Royal Windsor from 30 January to 3 February 2007 and then continued to Cheltenham, Milton Keynes, Richmond and Newcastle. Freeman was last on stage in October 2005, in Toby Whithouse's *Blue Eyes and Heels* at the Soho Theatre in London (aside from his guest role in *The Exonerated* at Riverside Studios in June 2006). By this point, his stage credits included such productions as *Kosher Harry, Jump Mr Malinoff, Jump* and *La Dispute*. Written by Richard Harris, *The Last Laugh* was adapted from an original play by Koki Mitani. Freeman plays a comedy writer who is forced by law to submit a script for government approval. The play follows the approval process.

Peter Lathan of the *British Theatre Guide* wrote of the play, '*The Last Laugh* is essentially a two-hander with Lloyd Pack (*Only Fools and Horses*) joined by Martin Freeman (*The Office*) as the Writer, and a nice cameo by Christopher Mellows as the Veteran. The performances are impeccable – even the timing of the badly timed gags is spot-on! It is played out in a large, cold, grey room which has clearly once been part of a library, designed by Michael Pavelka and subtly lit by Mark Henderson.'

Freeman was also seen in an episode of *Comedy Showcase* called 'Other People', which kicked off a run of six *Comedy Showcase* episodes. The programme ran from 2007 to 2012 and featured Britain's growing comedy talent. It was inspired by the long-running comedy-sketch anthology series of the 1960s' *Comedy Playhouse*.

In Martin's episode, which aired on 5 October 2007, he

plays Greg Wilson, a has-been child magician whose career crashed 1986 after he was humiliated on a children's phone-in show. In his thirties, Greg now works as a sofa salesman and is recognised by a former fan (Siobhan Finneran) and is asked for an autograph.

Freeman told *The Independent*'s James Rampton in 2007, 'When the woman in the furniture store asks for his autograph, he immediately obliges. It's a knee-jerk reaction. He thinks, "Someone wants me, I'm in the limelight again – even if only for two seconds." Once you've tasted the limelight, it's hard to let it go. Everyone wants to be acknowledged.'

The autograph request triggers a series of events, which ends up with Greg in a courtroom facing a sentence.

Martin said he could relate to his character because he knew what it felt like to have the weight of the world on his shoulders after he found success with *The Office*. Greg's desperate need to be famous is not something Freeman desires but rather a symptom of the modern world, as evidenced on such TV shows as *The X Factor*. Even when Greg's career went downhill, he was still hungry for fame.

Interestingly, Freeman believes that happy people do not make great comedy, as he explained at the time to *The Independent*'s James Rampton in 2007: 'Comedy can't be about continuous success. The characters we get behind – whether it's Hancock or Basil Fawlty or Captain Mainwaring – are eternally frustrated. Disappointment is an endless wellspring of comedy inspiration.'

British Comedy Guide wrote of the episode, 'We thought this pilot was brilliant – one of the best things we saw in 2007. As has been mentioned by a number of people in our forum, the episode delivered some really good laugh-out-loud moments. Nicholas Burns was particularly great as the mad lawyer. We'd love to see a full series of *Other People* but have come to accept that will never happen as it would be hard to convert the premise into a full series without overstretching it.'

Freeman was next seen on TV in December 2007 as Mr Codlin in *The Old Curiosity Shop*. Based on the Charles Dickens novel, the TV film stars Sophie Vavasseur as Nell Trent, Derek Jacobi as her grandfather and George MacKay as Nell's friend Kit Nubbles, as well as Zoë Wanamaker as Mrs Jarley, Toby Jones as Quilp, Adam Godley as Sampson Brass, Gina McKee as Sally Brass, Bryan Dick as Freddie Trent, Steve Pemberton as Mr Short, Josie Lawrence as Mrs Jiniwin, Bradley Walsh as Mr Liggers, Anna Madeley as Betsey Quilp, Geoff Breton as Dick Swiveller, Charlene McKenna as the Marchioness, Kelly Campbell as Mrs Nubbles, Katie Dunne as Baby Nubbles and Philip Noone as Rodney. It was broadcast on ITV on 26 December.

Martin was seen as himself in four episodes of *When Were We Funniest?* during the 2008 series. The comedy channel Gold got the public to decide which they thought was the funniest decade from the 1960s to the 2000s. But before the public voted, Gold picked five celebrities to represent each decade and encouraged them to convince the public that their decade was the funniest. The series kicked off with the celebrities on a panel explaining to the public why they should vote for their own decade. Each celebrity was given two episodes to convince the public. The outline was simple: in the first episode they explained why their decade was the funniest and used clips to highlight their argument and the public got to vote for the five funniest clips. In the second episode the clips were ordered according to public popularity, based on votes from the funniest to the least funny. The public were asked to vote for the most amusing decade and the funniest clip. The top five clips and the funniest decade was revealed in the final episode and the celebrities passed comments on their place in the vote. The series was narrated by Alexander Armstrong.

Trying his hand at something entirely different, Freeman next took part in two films as Rembrandt in the 2007 narrative film *Nightwatching* and 2008's documentary film *Rembrandt's J'Accuse*. They are both joint Dutch, German and Finnish documentaries directed by Peter Greenaway and were released a year apart, and feature many of the same actors and sets. The films explore the two sides of Rembrandt's romantic and professional life and the controversy surrounding the identification of a murderer in his painting 'The Night Watch'. Rembrandt's use of shadow, light and colour was a major source of inspiration to Greenaway. 'The Night Watch' itself hangs in the Rijksmuseum in Amsterdam. The film covers the period of Rembrandt's life in which his wife Saskia, and mother to his son Titus, dies. He then starts a self-destructive relationship with his housekeeper before moving on to another member of his housekeeping crew, who is twenty years old.

Freeman was very proud to be in the two films and the process was not something he'd experienced before. He usually gets roles about lovelorn middle-aged Surrey men, so to play a Dutch master of art was an opportunity he could not resist and working with Peter Greenaway was an opportunity not to be overlooked, especially at that stage in his career. He hoped that films such as *The All Together* and *Nightwatching* would knock away his nice-guy-next-door persona once and for all. Working with Greenaway was an opportunity that he simply could not refuse and Martin was most impressed by the films.

'I just hope that when you see it you get as much of the story across as I got from reading it. Not all Peter's stuff is sequential, narrative story,' the actor admitted to *Indie London.co.uk*'s Rob Carnevale. 'Some of it is like an art installation and I'm not particularly interested in being in an art installation to be honest. I'm interested in the story and it was a story. So I hope that it's intact when I see the film properly – that there is a beginning, a middle and an end. Sometimes that can easily be overlooked for the sake of cleverness. But story, for me, is really, really important whether it's *Red Riding Hood* or *The Godfather*. Everything else has to defer to that.'

Making *Nightwatching* was not an easy experience though. Freeman rang his fellow *The Good Night* actor Michael Gambon, who had also starred in *The Cook, The Thief, His Wife & Her Lover*, which Greenaway directed, for any advice or tips. Gambon apparently said that Greenaway leaves you alone. He does not presume to tell you how to act. He directs from a distance, but he is specific about what he wants. He's less hands-on with his actors than he is with the crew because everything in the shot, in front of the camera, governs the progress of the film.

Freeman spoke to *Ain't It Cool*'s Capone about his experiences: 'Well, it wasn't intimidating, but it wasn't easy either. I don't think there's anything about him that is easy, to be honest. Not that he's a difficult man. I never found that he was weird or difficult with me, but his films aren't easy, obviously, and his films are always pretty challenging.'

Martin continued to explain what it was like working with Greenaway: 'The process that he puts you through is fairly challenging, because as an actor, obviously, you're used to waiting for the lighting, but you're not used to waiting that long for the lighting, you know. You're not used to waiting, like, half the day for the scene to be lit, but that's, of course, what gives his films their look. That's why his films are unique, because they look the way they do. I'm playing Rembrandt at the heart of this film, and there has to be a sort of human, beating heart at the core of the movie the rest of the film can sort of exist around. And, he's a very hands-off director, you know. He leaves you alone.'

Nightwatching received mostly passable reviews, though critics praised Freeman's superb performance.

'Often, Greenaway's handling of actors is his weakest point: but he gets fiercely intelligent performances here from Martin Freeman and Eva Birthistle as the artist and his wife Saskia,' wrote Peter Bradshaw of *The Guardian*. 'Greenaway's group compositions are bracingly cerebral – and sometimes very erotic. His tableaux vivants are like glittering 21st-century cine-masques, with a poetic structure which swerves conventional expectations of location and narrative.'

Empire's Adam Smith penned a review that said, 'Martin Freeman is outstanding as the lusty young genius who, when commissioned to paint members of the Amsterdam militia in their finery, instead produces a portrait packed with half-hidden insults and an accusation of murder.'

The Independent's Anthony Quinn said, 'Unfortunately, this art history lesson is enclosed within a two-hour movie of near-stupefying tedium. Martin Freeman, stocky and stubbly, is not bad at all as the outspoken artist, and his grief over his dying wife Saskia (Eva Birthistle) is made convincingly raw.'

Writing in *Variety*, Jay Weissberg said, 'Freeman, best known for the UK series *The Office*, is just the man, inhabiting the foul-mouthed, lusty artist and making him believable rather than theatrical. Birthistle and May are also standouts, rising to the challenge of being flesh and blood amid the stagecraft. Non-English thespers are less successful, made to recite long, explanatory dialogue that's difficult to decipher under the thick accents. Multitude of players gets lost as Greenaway seems uncertain which elements to focus on at what moment, leaving a disjointed sense that's not helped by a choppy feel for time's passing.'

There were other directors Freeman had a desire to work with. Notably, Francis Ford Coppola, as Freeman is a huge fan of *The Godfather* films, and then there's Spike Lee, Ken Loach and Shane Meadows. These directors are auteur film-makers whose body of work carries particular themes which are personal to them – for example Coppola's Italian-American background or Meadows's working-class roots – and there's an individual style to each of the director's works. Of course, he wouldn't turn down the chance of working with Steven Spielberg either. Freeman even met director and master puppeteer Frank Oz once and wouldn't say no to the opportunity of working with him either. Speaking to *IndieLondon.co.uk* in 2007, Freeman said, 'There's also never been a better film than the first two

Godfathers, so I'd love to work with Coppola. I'd also like to work with his daughter because I think she's fucking serious, really serious. But I think there are a lot of people. I met Frank Oz last year and really liked him. He's a really lovely director as well. Spielberg's not bad at all [laughs].'

To celebrate the fiftieth anniversary of Motown Records Freeman hosted a special edition of BBC2's *The Culture Show*, which was first broadcast in March 2009. In the programme he visits both Detroit and LA and charts the story of soul and motown, his favourite type of music. As a self-confessed anorak, it was a joy for Freeman to visit some of his heroes. In Detroit he speaks to the last surviving member of the Four Tops, Duke Fakir, and Sylvia Moy, who wrote 'Uptight' for Stevie Wonder, motown producer Clay McMurray, who worked in Quality Control for Motown Records and vied for the release of Stevie Wonder's 'My Cherie Amour'. He also chatted to DJ Scottie Regan, who played motown on white radio stations and introduced the music to a new generation of fans. He spoke to the legendary Martha Reeves of Martha and The Vandellas, who later became a Detroit councillor. He also got to interview guitarist Eddie Willis, bass player Bob Babbitt and drummer Uriel Jones, three original members of the Funk Brothers who helped shape the sound of 1960s motown. He then journeys to LA to chart the story of the label, as Motown Records moved to the City of Angels in 1972. He interviews three members of The Jackson 5: Marlon, Tito and Jackie, along with Mary Wilson of The Supremes and Otis Williams of The Temptations, as well as songwriters Lamont Dozier and Brian and Eddie Holland, whose hits include 'Where Did Our Love Go' and 'Reach Out'.

Although many of his favourite artists are black American soul singers, he has a firm grasp on contemporary British music, with his favourite bands of the day being Super Furry Animals, The Bees, The Coral and The Zutons.

Freeman next starred in the four-part drama *Boy Meets Girl*. It was slightly different from what he had done in the past, so he was open to a new challenge.

Martin stars as Danny Reed, who is struck by lightning only to wake up and find he is inside the body of a woman – fashion journalist Veronica Burton, played by Rachel Stirling. Veronica has a busy social life, is financially stable and has a devoted boyfriend called Jay, played by Paterson Joseph. Danny is tired of life and directionless and takes out his frustration on his customers at the DIY store where he works. He pines for his co-worker Fiona (played by Angela Griffin) and tells of his encyclopaedic knowledge of pointless information to his good friend Pete (Marshall Lancaster). So the freakish accident that causes him to swap bodies with Veronica turns his life upside down. They both struggle with their new identities and learn some new truths about themselves. However, by the end of the series they long to get back to their own bodies and their own lives.

Speaking about their preparation for the roles, Rachel Stirling told *British Comedy Guide*, 'I watched everything that featured transgender roles, but I have also now played four male parts in my career. Martin and I worked incredibly hard at getting the right physicality and the right voices. We videotaped each other and copied each other's mannerisms.

Waking up in someone else's body would be a nightmare and I hope we've told that story.'

The pair were not around each other much on set because their scenes were filmed separately. They recorded each other's acting scenes so they could watch them and pick up on each other's mannerisms and such. Acting is about observation as much as anything else; watching people talk, listening to them and paying attention to your surroundings is vital to an actor's research.

'Martin and I studied each other like apes,' Stirling told *The Independent*'s James Rampton. 'Like a lot of actors, he's quite a feminine, sensitive man, and I'm quite a masculine woman, so we could steal bits off each other. I videoed Martin performing a scene as me and nicked some of his mannerisms.'

Freeman had a few meetings with an acting teacher to give him some tips about female physicality and how it is different from male physicality. The way a woman talks, carries herself and sits down was important to Freeman's preparation for the part.

'Voice projection is very different,' he told *British Comedy Guide*, 'and it's very easy to get it wrong and end up being a bit too panto. It was very helpful to have someone say put your chin down, make your chest softer, use your head less and use your eyes more, because those are little clues that I wouldn't necessarily have picked up on.'

He observed the way a woman picks up a wine glass with her fingertips rather than the palm of her hands, for example, and how women don't stare at men, whereas men are not bothered at all who notices them. These little differences in gender, generally speaking, were helpful.

'It's not as though I didn't have a camp bone in my body beforehand,' he joked to *The Independent*'s James Rampton. 'I'm an actor, for goodness' sake! As an actor, you learn to deal with mockery, as most people think it's not a very manly job. But fortunately, as Adam Ant so aptly put it, ridicule is nothing to be scared of.'

The series' key point is how we are defined by the way we look. Freeman and Stirling excel on screen together. They have charisma, charm and chemistry.

'It doesn't have any of the clichés of gender swapping dramas,' Freeman said to *Last Broadcast*. 'It could have been quite facile but I think it works because I've got a bit of femininity about me and Rachael has a bit of boyishness about her.'

Co-star Paterson Joseph told Michael Deacon of the *Daily Telegraph*, 'The script was hilarious but when we came to do it, I realised how horrible this was: it was like having somebody with Alzheimer's in your life. There's a scene where she pushes me around, and it was frightening. So it keeps a balance between a situation comedy and a painful, dysfunctional drama.'

Boy Meets Girl ran for four episodes and began on 1 May 2009. Little has been mentioned of it since.

John Preston panned the series in his review in the *Daily Telegraph*: 'Many theories have been put forward as to why Michael Grade is stepping down as Executive Chairman of ITV. But I'm beginning to suspect I know the real answer. Someone hovering above him in the hierarchy must have seen *Boy Meets Girl* (Friday, ITV1) and decided that this couldn't be allowed to go on.'

The *Daily Mirror*'s Jane Simon observed, 'Although Martin

Freeman is the better known of the two, it's Stirling – best known for her role in *Tipping The Velvet* as well as for being Diana Rigg's daughter – who gets the lion's share of screen time in this first episode.'

A bit of a history buff, Freeman wanted to learn some of the truths of his family, as he told *Wales Online*: 'A member of my family had a go once. It's really difficult to do, and the problem is, you end up with a kind of theory or a half truth. People then end up falling in love with that theory, but the difficulty comes when it's not necessarily the truth. It's good to let an expert do it for you.'

In the space of just a few short weeks he went from knowing almost nothing about the history of his family to knowing a series of important events dating back more than a hundred years.

He continued, 'I hoped we would cover my grandparents, and from watching the show previously I knew it was possible to find out about great-grandparents and even further in some cases.'

It took time for all the newly acquired knowledge to sink into his system. He discovered members of his family faced great adversities and he was impressed by their strength of spirit and character in how they dealt with such terrible issues.

That same year he was also seen as Chris Curry in the TV film *Micro Men*, which was originally broadcast on 8 October on BBC4. *Micro Men* is a one-off TV film set in the late 1970s and early to mid-1980s and concerns the rivalry between ZX Spectrum developer Sir Clive Sinclair (Alexander Armstrong) and Chris Curry (Freeman), who created the BBC Micro.

'I didn't think computers would take off,' Freeman, a technophobe, told *The Scotsman* in 2009. 'But this was more about these two men and their rivalry. It's so easy and compulsory to laugh when you see Clive Sinclair being interviewed because he is a bizarre figure, but he kick-started a lot of stuff and I came away with an admiration.'

The film's central story is about the rise of the British PC market as the two rivalries compete to become the provider of a home computer for the BBC's programming for schools. The film mixes fact with fiction for dramatic effect.

Den Of Geek's Aaron Birch wrote, 'Armstrong's portrayal of Clive Sinclair as a tyrannical, yet brilliant inventor is spot on, and Freeman's far more down-to-earth outing as Curry helps to deliver the confrontational head-banging between the two clashing personalities. What we have here, though, is not simply an affectionate portrayal of the computing giants, but also an intriguing and accurate look into the growth of the now enormous industry, an industry that the UK helped to launch.'

Never one to shy away from trying out new endeavours, Freeman returned to short films to star in *HIV: The Musical* alongside Julian Barratt, Seb Cardinal and Dustin Demri-Burns. Made for around £4,000 it was released in October 2009.

He then played Paul Maddens in the film *Nativity!* directed by *Confetti* director Debbie Isitt and released on 29 November 2009. The film was partly improvised, whereas *Confetti* was fully improvised, and stars Freeman as Paul Maddens, a primary-school teacher who attempts to produce and direct a nativity play that will outdo a competing school. Jason Watkins, Ashley Jensen, Marc Wotton, Alan Carr, Ricky Tomlinson, Pam Ferris and Clarke Peters also star in the production.

Freeman thinks the nativity tale is a great story and a grand tradition, so it was something that he was not going to turn down. He's fascinated by the myth and truth behind the nativity story. Whether you believe it is true or not, there is a reason why it is called 'The Greatest Story Ever Told' and Freeman was not swayed by any religious reasons; he just thought it was a beautiful story. He told *The Scotsman* in 2009: 'Organised religion, organised anything, requires commitment and requires an engagement with something. A lot of the time, we don't want to commit. Of course, if you talk about the Spanish Inquisition, that's the bad end of organised religion. But organised means there's more than ten people involved, because it was an idea people liked. I don't see how you get round it.'

One comparison had been made between Freeman's character and his pupils with Jesus and his disciples. 'I hadn't seen it like that,' he responded to a journalist at *Inspire Magazine*, 'but the reason for me that any of that stuff, the religiosity, has validity is that there are some quite good ideas and some quite good things to give to people – like the idea of redemption; the idea that we can turn something around. We don't even see those things in religious terms. They are human things, they are part of our language and our culture.'

He continued, 'If we are watching films who do we get behind? The underdog. What the flip was Jesus if he wasn't an underdog, born in a bleedin' manger, you know what I mean? I've always loved the story because of that. Because whether you believe or not, that is a more succinct lesson about how we should be looking at the world than anything else. The trouble is we stop looking at the world like that when we take it out of that context. We don't then look at a homeless person and think "what can I do for you?" we think he must deserve it in some way. It's hard to take out those parallels from something specific and put them into the wider world.'

The British nativity play at the end of the year nearing Christmas is sort of like the American high-school musical but much less glamorous and more accessible. The children are not little Hollywood stars; in the film the viewer gets to see the kids messing up and falling around. The idea for the film was to make it children-friendly, which Isitt was adamant about. Freeman was not at all concerned about being upstaged by children.

The actor says he doesn't just turn up on set and act; there is a process. If it looks effortless on-screen, he's evidently done his job.

'I'm not interested in, "What can I do to impress?"' he admitted to *The Guardian*'s Alice Wignall in 2009. 'Well, play the role. I hate it when people show you what they're doing. No one wants to see the cogs. But very often that's what's lauded as great acting: "Look at me working! Look at my false nose!"'

Because the script was improvised and Freeman swears so much, the director had to keep reminding him that it was a children's film. Martin concluded that he would not have the patience or tolerance to be a teacher in real life. Those high-pitched shouts at the start of the film came from his own experiences as a father. *Peep Show*'s Robert Webb does not have fond memories of the filming: 'just an unhappy experience,' he said to *The Guardian*'s Alexis Petridis. 'Improvising, in May, while naked, standing around in a garden. So cold.'

Freeman, however, enjoyed working with Debbie Isitt, otherwise he would not have gone back for *Nativity!*.

Watching school plays can often be a cringe-worthy experience but as a parent there is something very forgivable and enjoyable about it. There's an innocence about seeing children doing their best and having fun with acting. That's partly why Freeman was attracted to the film's premise. It's real, the kids are not pretending to be kids. They're doing their best and there's something very moving and emotional about that.

The process of making *Confetti* was less explained. The actors could go in any direction they liked, within reason and as long as it led the story in the right direction.

'… it was more "you have to get from A to Z, saying this, we need to plot that, and at some point someone needs to say that,"' Freeman explained to *Future Movies.co.uk*'s Paul Gallagher about *Nativity!*, 'Debbie likes the uncertainty, and I think she has enough respect for actors, as good a screenwriter as she is, and she likes to let unexpected things happen that may be, hopefully, better than what she would have had in mind.'

They had to rehearse a great deal more than what is shown in the final film. They spent hours going through the choreography and rehearsing the songs. During some stints in filming Freeman tried to appeal to the older children to set a good example and, at times, it worked but there were some points during this time when the children were just being children and messing about.

The film was released only in the UK and was a surprise success, both critically and commercially, and has since become something of a cult classic of its kind.

There is much cynicism in America – especially Middle America – about non-domestic films, which is frustrating for an actor such as Freeman. But it is a huge country where there is plenty of money to be made.

Tim Robey wrote in his lukewarm review in the *Daily Telegraph* '… it improves, big-time, partly because Freeman and Jensen play the pathos so well, and partly because the actual show is a genuine delight, catchily penned by Isitt herself, and asking the kids to be kids, in all their cloying, charming, Britain's Got Not Enough Talent glory.'

The Guardian's Jason Solomons wrote, 'Another British comedy limps into cinemas having inexplicably wrestled its way out of a television script meeting. Martin Freeman deserves an endurance medal for helping this over the finish line as primary school teacher and failed actor Mr Maddens, who puts on a musical nativity play after promising his ex-girlfriend will be coming from Hollywood to Coventry to see it.'

A sequel called *Nativity 2: Danger in the Manger* was released in 2012 and a third film began filming in 2013. Neither of these star Freeman.

Martin was working obsessively by this point and, given the comfortable state of his finances, had the option of taking a break if he'd so wished. There weren't that many scripts that he liked and he has always been picky about which ones he wants to commit to. He had built up a steady stream of acting credentials in both film and TV. He was becoming more recognised as each year passed but the roles he took did not dispel the notion in many people's minds that he was still 'Tim from *The Office*'.

'*The Office* is mostly what people recognise me from,' he said to *The Scotsman* at the time, 'and I'm only glad that it wasn't as a murderer in a soap that I became famous. But it's a bit disconcerting when you read about yourself in the newspaper and it says, "This is what Tim did next," and people think I am going to be avuncular and jovial when they meet me because that's the way Tim was in *The Office*.'

Freeman had finally given in and hired an American agent to look after his affairs in LA. For years he had resisted and been a little suspicious about Hollywood, given its reputation as a fickle town of faded hopes and dreams, but he accepted that there was certainly a great deal more work available in the US than in his native UK. Success in America could make a major difference to any actor's career.

'Obviously, there are also people in America that I absolutely love,' he admitted to BBC Movies' Rob Carnevale on the subject.

He'd certainly made the right decisions switching to more dramatic roles in recent years in the UK and, with a hired hand over in the States, his sights were set high. Freeman does not equate money with success. 'If an actor has a huge bank balance and fifty-three cars, good for them,' he told Andrew Duncan of *Reader's Digest*. 'They're a great business person, but their work may mean nothing. I have much more in common with Tom Courtenay – one of the people who made me want to act as a kid – than someone who can buy planet earth four times over.'

With such varied roles to his name, Freeman was soon to be cast in one of the most famous roles in the whole of English literature, which would turn around his career and make him one of the most well-known actors in Britain, but not before another home-grown success hit the UK's screens.

CHAPTER SIX

SHERLOCK HOLMES AND DOCTOR WATSON

'The loudest, friendliest and most enthusiastic part of our fan base seems to be teenage girls between college and university age, but that surprised me, actually.'
FREEMAN TALKING TO MARK GATISS IN THE *RADIO TIMES*, 2014

'To be honest, I don't really know what that means,' he said to the *Sunday Times*'s Benji Wilson. 'It's like when people say something is quintessentially English. I don't think the people saying it know what it means, either.'

'It sounds like a backhanded compliment, because I think, "What, you don't think I'm exciting? You don't think I'm dangerous?"' he later elaborated to Josh Rottenberg of *Entertainment Weekly*. 'Any pigeonhole is something to be rebelled against. When people say, "You're a normal Everyman," I go, "Well, you fucking find five of me in the street then! There aren't many of me walking around, you know!"'

On the plus side, had he played a villain in a TV soap, strangers may not have been so nice to him when they approached him in the street. It's often the case that members of the public forget that there's a line between fiction and reality and what an actor may be like on camera is not necessarily how they are in real life. Most of Freeman's fans and admirers were courteous and polite.

His most successful roles, however, were just around the corner.

'If someone had a pint with me, they'd find out pretty quickly I'm not so nice,' he confessed to *The Independent*'s Emma Jones in 2013. 'I'm not Tim from *The Office*, although a lot of people still think I am. I have absolutely no problem telling someone to fuck off.'

He becomes infuriated when people think he can only play one character and that's himself. He's done much to dispel that misconceived notion since *The Office*, as he explained to Alice Wignall of *The Guardian* in 2009: 'If you mean I look a bit like him and I sound a bit like him – yeah, that's because I'm playing him and it didn't say "He's Somalian" on the script, otherwise I would have tried an accent. If the script says, "Guy in his 30s, my generation, lives in England" what am I going to do? Start acting like I'm half-lizard? There's no point, because no one wants to see it.'

Freeman was cast as the legendary Doctor John Watson in the acclaimed BBC drama *Sherlock* with Benedict Cumberbatch. He knew it would be a success from the get-go, as he told *The Guardian*'s Euan Ferguson: 'Look, it sounds arrogant to hell, but I remember reading an *NME* interview with McCartney and they'd been in Abbey Road, doing *Sgt Pepper*, when everyone was saying. "What's happened to the Beatles?" and it was, "Just you wait, just you fucking wait until this comes out." Same thing happened. I knew it was great, writing great, Benedict fucking great… I really must stop swearing.'

Sherlock came around at the right time. The roles that he was getting offered were much less exciting and, although he was famous as a result of his role in *The Hitchhiker's Guide to the Galaxy*, there was a point when it caused him to worry about his talent. Freeman even asked a friend of his if he thought he was a good actor, but then he simply accepted another part and moved on. He was living in a new house said to be worth £900,000, in Hertfordshire near his birthplace in Aldershot, on the outskirts of London, with his partner Abbie Abbington and their two children Joe and Grace, who was born in 2008, and he had a huge tax bill to pay so it was important to keep busy.

Aldershot is a quiet leafy area that is a far cry from the busy suburbs of his previous home in Potters Bar, Crouch End and, before then, Bethnal Green – but he moved from there in 1993 when the BNP were voted in. As a leftie, Freeman believes that the term 'multiculturalism' polarises people – and that we shouldn't notice what ethnicity a person is. People are people regardless of their ethnic background.

'There is no country in the world like this,' he told Chris Sullivan of the *Daily Mail*. 'If all of a sudden all the traffic wardens in Ghana were Welsh, they'd really notice and might not love it? We give ourselves a hard time in this country in a sort of mea culpa way. But if we were that racist, people wouldn't come. Very simple.'

Things have not changed all that much for him since he found fame. He's got an extensive DVD library, a precious record collection, dislikes computers and still prefers his agent to send him scripts by post rather than email. He is not a fan of social media either. He loves clothes and fashion and, being a fastidious dresser, drives his partner crazy when he pulls out the ironing board just to nip to the shops.

He's never learned to drive because he thinks there are better things to spend his money on – such as clothes and records.

Freeman is a family man. Despite his wealth, success and growing critical stature, he is a father first and foremost and has succeeded thus far in keeping his children out of the limelight. 'Obviously they're what I'm proudest of, but when I grew up I thought all actors were [private] like De Niro,' he said to *Reader's Digest*'s Andrew Duncan. 'All I've read about him is that he likes black women. These days you have to know everything, and it's tedious.'

When asked if his tiny long-haired dog Archie compromises his manliness, he replied to *Metro* journalist Andrew Williams about the family dachshund, 'Occasionally. Fortunately though I am already an actor and wear nicely tailored coats, so it doesn't make much difference. It can get a bit too much though. One day recently I was wearing quite a poncey coat and walking Archie around Old Compton Street and suddenly thought "Oh Christ!" I felt like such a lord. Where would fashion be without the feminine touch, though? You need that in art, fashion, everything. No one I know is a jock, I don't have any jock friends, that's why I went into fucking acting to begin with.'

Curiously, Freeman and Abbington have not chosen to marry and Abbington admits that she is not sure why. 'We don't want to spoil it. We've got two children together, two dogs and a cat and a house, and that's such a big commitment,' she said to the *Daily Mail*'s Vicki Power in 2011. 'Maybe one day we will, but we wouldn't want a huge hoopla; we'd run away and do it on our own and have a party afterwards.'

The one downer for Freeman of being so busy in both his personal and professional life is that he finds little time to make it to the country – notably, to his native Hampshire, as he explained to *Hampshire Life*'s Frank Grice: 'I don't make it back to Hampshire an awful lot. I'd rather have my family come to me if at all possible. But I love the times when I am back in the county. The peace and pace of the countryside – it's incredibly nurturing and therapeutic for me. That's really not one of those things you can search out and find. It has to be special to you.'

The *Sherlock* series was created by Steven Moffat and Mark Gatiss, both of whom had prior experience with adapting Victorian literature. Moffat had adapted *The Strange Case of Dr Jekyll and Mr Hyde* in 2007 for the series *Jekyll*, while noted writer and actor Gatiss had penned the Dickensian *Doctor Who* episode 'The Unquiet Dead'. They had discussed the idea of a Sherlock Holmes adaptation on various train journeys to Cardiff, where *Doctor Who* is filmed. They finally decided to go ahead with the idea after Moffat's wife, producer Sue Vertue, encouraged them to develop the project while they were away at an awards show in Monte Carlo. Moffat and Gatiss roped in writer Stephen Thompson in September 2008. It was then just a matter of casting.

Moffat and Vertue were keen to cast Cumberbatch after seeing him the 2007 film *Atonement*. He did a brilliant audition for the creative team – his voice, look and attitude was perfect for the role of Holmes, who is far from your everyday person.

The creative team admitted that Cumberbatch was the only actor they originally envisaged for Holmes and discovered that finding the right actor to play Watson was a far more difficult task. Of course, they had to find not only someone who could play Watson to a T but an actor who had on-screen chemistry with Cumberbatch. Matt Smith reportedly auditioned for Watson but was turned down and later cast by Moffat as the eleventh *Doctor Who*. Ironically, Freeman is reported to have been considered for *Doctor Who* at one point as a successor to David Tennant but Smith got the gig.

'The points for it would have been that it would have been a laugh being Doctor Who, plus the money,' Freeman told *The Scotsman*. 'But against that would have been being on jigsaw puzzles and lunch boxes.'

Martin was admittedly dubious about the idea of updating Holmes for the twenty-first century but, as one of the writers pointed out, each of Ian Fleming's James Bond novels had been updated, so why would it not work with Conan Doyle's Sherlock Holmes stories? Freeman did not like the idea that it would pretend to be 'cool' but by page two of the script he was hooked.

'I was sent the script,' Martin told Mark Gatiss in a special feature for the *Radio Times*. 'When I was told there was going to be an updated Sherlock Holmes, I thought, "That could be risky, but it's going to be Steven Moffat and Mark Gatiss, so OK – show it to me!" So I went in for it. But it's probably fair to say I wasn't in the best frame of mind.' Freeman added, 'A week later my agent rang and said, "Listen, this *Sherlock* thing, they're sort of under the impression you weren't that into it."

And I said, "Oh... I am really interested. Please call them and let them know that I am interested." I wasn't being blasé about it at all. I just wasn't on my best day. So I came in again, read with Benedict and it instantly worked, it seemed to me. I always liked Ben's work. I thought he was a fantastic actor and there was something about our rhythms, similarities and differences that meant that it just happened.'

The reason why the creative team assumed Freeman was not really interested in the part was because his initial interview and audition with them did not go down so well. Freeman had had his wallet stolen on the way to the meeting, which infuriated him.

He told the *Daily Telegraph*'s Craig McLean about the audition, 'I know I was in a bad mood. And I'm sometimes not very good at hiding that. So I wasn't really doing the dance. And that was probably being reflected back at me in the audition.'

Freeman read for them again and read with Cumberbatch and it went down a storm and that's what won it for him – his chemistry with his fellow lead actor. Cumberbatch has a very assured way with words and is excellent at handling mercurial, eccentric characters.

'We had seen a lot of very good people, but when we paired Martin with Benedict it was stellar instantly, you could see the show,' said Moffat to *The Guardian*'s John Plunkett. 'Martin is very responsive to the performances around him and once they started bouncing off each other, I said to Mark, "That's the show right there."'

As a fan of the Big Smoke, Freeman was keen to see the city shown in all its beauty in front of the camera – after all

Sherlock Holmes is to London what Philip Marlowe is to Los Angeles in Raymond Chandler's gritty noir novels.

'And it's that whole London thing, isn't it – it's the thrill of doing something that is pivotal to the artistic history of this great city,' he said to Anthony Pearce of *London Calling.com*. 'When you get to explore something like that, I feel it makes it even more special.'

In the series, after coming back from Afghanistan, Watson is damaged both internally and externally and, upon meeting Holmes, he is introduced to a far more exciting world than he was living as a civilian. Holmes takes him away from his books and laptop and offers him something challenging and fun.

The Scottish-born writer and physician Sir Arthur Conan Doyle based Sherlock Holmes on Dr Joseph Bell, who was a surgeon at the Royal Infirmary of Edinburgh. Doyle worked for Bell as a clerk and was mesmerised by his powers of deduction. Holmes first appeared in print in 1887 with the publication of the novel *A Study in Scarlet*, which first appeared in *Beeton's Christmas Annual*. In total, Doyle wrote four novels and fifty-six short stories stretching to 1927. Only four of the stories are not narrated by Watson – 'The Adventure of the Blanched Soldier' and 'The Adventure of the Lion's Mare' are narrated by Holmes, while 'The Adventure of the Musgrave Ritual' and 'The Adventure of the Gloria Scott' are written in the third person.

The friendship and love between Holmes and Watson is what appealed to Moffat and Gatiss as they developed the characters for the new version of the Conan Doyle stories. They did not want Watson to come across as the bumbling idiot that

Nigel Bruce portrayed him as in the Basil Rathbone adaptions. Watson comes across as a more down-to-earth character in the latest adaptation; someone who humbles Holmes and acts as his moral compass, as some of the things Holmes does are certainly morally dubious. Colin Blakely, in Billy Wilder's 1970 film *The Private Life of Sherlock Holmes*, was an influence on the new version. David Burke and Raymond Francis have also portrayed Watson in the past.

Freeman spoke to *Den of Geek*'s Louisa Mellor about the various on-screen incarnations: 'The ITV ones in the eighties and the nineties with Jeremy Brett were fantastic, they were really really fantastic and I occasionally watch them now when they're on and am amazed still by how well they hold up, they're really good pieces of work. But this is contemporary, that's not been done for ages.'

He continued, 'Benedict's a very good Sherlock. He looks like Sherlock Holmes, he sounds like Sherlock Holmes, he's really good. I suppose they've highlighted the relationship between Sherlock and John more than many others. I think John is less of a passenger in this than he has been in other incarnations. That in itself wouldn't necessarily make it more popular, but I think people like to see two people having to rub up against each other and find their way around life. I like the friendly conflict between them.'

Freeman also listened to the audio tapes of the original stories through his iPod but, ultimately, he bases his acting for the part on what the script dictates.

As Watson, Martin Freeman is the everyday bloke to Sherlock's eccentric, quirky character. Watson is the teller of stories; a wordsmith but with a common touch. There is a humanity about him, which stems from his background in war. As much as Freeman may loathe the label, he is the sort of bloke one could meet in the street and converse with. Whereas Sherlock attracts the wrong sort of attention, Watson is approachable. Sidekicks in any medium – from TV to film to comic books and literature – tend to be seen as cringe-worthy characters, from Tonto, The Lone Ranger's accomplice, to Batman's younger apprentice, Robin. There have been many different incarnations of Watson, some of which have been played straight and others for laughs.

The writers, Moffat and Gatiss, were respectful to Conan Doyle's creation and avoided patronising Watson. In a way, they created Watson as a hardly human character, as they did Holmes. Watson himself is a man of unfathomable intellect and enjoys his own shrewd powers of determination. He also knows how to deal with Holmes, who has a talent that most people don't possess and a personality that many people would struggle to deal with. It's a self-reverential show and, in some respects, it's surprising how well the writers have pulled off a modern-day adaptation. The original stories were written over a hundred years ago but the new series has a place in the modern world. Conan Doyle feels present in the writing because Moffat and Gatiss are so respectful of his work. Freeman tried it like a new script that no one had ever filmed before.

'I think you can get into a lot of trouble if you try to hang your hat too much on what other people have done,' Freeman explained to *Wales Online*. 'It's just not your job. Those people haven't done this script. We're not playing the novels, we're not playing the films, we're doing this script by Stephen Moffat and Mark Gatiss.'

Martin had not read any of the Conan Doyle stories but was familiar with the Basil Rathbone and Nigel Bruce films because BBC2 used to show them in the early evenings back in the 1970s and 1980s when he was a teenager. As soon as he got the acting gig though, he devoured the stories. What Freeman enjoyed about the script was that it was not a comedy, yet there is much understated humour in the characters of Holmes and Watson. It's not played for laughs by any means but there are laughs to be found. Freeman's aim with Watson was to make him strong yet vulnerable and relatable.

Speaking to Andrew Duncan of *Reader's Digest* about Sherlock and his partner, Freeman said, 'John Watson is very pukka and traditional and lends a moral framework to Sherlock, who's more interested in the chase than in what's right or wrong.'

It was announced at the 2008 Edinburgh International Television Festival that the BBC were producing a single sixty-minute production of *Sherlock*. The cost of the production, as reported in *The Guardian*, was said to have been £800,000 and there were whispers that it would be a failure, so the pilot was not aired and, instead, the BBC requested reshoots leading to three ninety-minute episodes. The original pilot was later included on the DVD of the first series. It is almost entirely different from the broadcasted version, both in look and sound. The overall cost of the first series of *Sherlock* came in at a reported £1 million.

Filming for the pilot began in January 2008, while the first series of three episodes began filming in January 2010. There is a fantastically fresh look to the series with the location and setting. Much of the filming was done in Cardiff, which proved cheaper and provided some wonderful shots for a makeshift Victorian London. The wonderful score by David Arnold and Michael Price also added richness to the series.

Sherlock is set in contemporary London with Holmes as a consulting detective who solves cases with his flatmate and friend Watson, who has returned from military service in Afghanistan with the Royal Army Medical Corps. Holmes does not immediately win over the officers of the London Met, especially Detective Inspector Greg Lestrade, played by Rupert Graves. However, in time, due to his immense intellect and powers of observation and perception, he convinces them of his worth to the police force. Watson documents his adventures with Holmes on his blog, which makes Holmes an unlikely and reluctant celebrity. His odd personal life and his eccentric character make him fodder for the British press. He is soon asked by ordinary people and the British Government for help with various cases and mysteries. Throughout the series he meets his arch nemesis and rival, Jim Moriarty, played by Andrew Scott. Holmes is also infrequently assisted on some cases by Molly Hooper (Louise Brealey), a pathologist at St Bartholomew's Hospital. Una Stubbs plays Mrs Hudson, Holmes and Watson's landlady, while co-creator and writer Mark Gatiss is Holmes's elder brother, government official Mycroft.

What's fun about the show is that Holmes uses modern technology such as texting, the Internet and GPS to help crack cases. The writers update some of the traditional elements of the original Conan Doyle stories, such as character names and certain plot devices, as well as the 221B Baker Street address and such but they also add some of their own elements to make it more contemporary and plausible.

Cumberbatch spoke to *Den of Geek* about how technology aids modern policing: 'His mode of operation is aided by technology. His speciality is deducing the facts, which means pulling together a huge, vast amalgam of information into a coherent structure. So, he can understand what he sees, and experience what the story might be, what's not apparent to everybody.' He continued, 'Sometimes that catches him out. He can pre-empt things, and that can get him into trouble. He can go down blind alleys. He still, humanly, gets things wrong when he first meets Watson. He is fallible, but he completely fits in with the modern world of high tech, modern policing. He's a man who assimilates all that information, and builds a bigger picture out of it. And that's a very human thing to do. No machine can do that.'

Freeman was a little dubious about the tone of the show, worrying that viewers might be overloaded with too many computers and mobile phones and other modern-day technological devices. He was concerned that they might stray too far from the original source material. He was pleased that the writers managed to achieve a balance. It's all down to good writing at the end of the day. In fact, not even good but brilliant writing. If the script is quite good, there is a chance the episode or film can be a reasonable standard but, if the script is brilliant, it can be masterful.

'It's very much our thing,' Freeman said to the *University Observer*'s Steven Balbirnie, 'but as far as the spirit and the dynamic goes between those two characters, which is after all, really the success of the show, it's written that way, it's made that way, that you want to know about the dynamic of these two characters and that I think is true to Conan Doyle.'

On a personal level, Freeman is less pleased with technology, as he told Martina Fowler of *TV Choice Magazine*: 'I think the world's too computerised. Obviously I wouldn't go back to the fifties. I just spend a lot of time with people who should know better, who are really into gadgets. I just think, "Come on man, I know it's clever, but you're going to be getting rid of that in six months." We've all become so acclimatised to thinking, "OK, I'm supposed to buy that now." We're all intelligent people, why are we going along with this?'

Martin thinks that Watson has an understated dress sense. Holmes's friend is often seen wearing smart casual clothes but he doesn't have the sartorial obsession that Freeman has. The actor has admitted he probably spends more time getting ready than his partner does. He doesn't have any grooming products but he has always loved clothes.

Freeman flourishes in the role. He brings out Watson's main traits: his iron-willed character, his strong mindedness, his sense of morality and decorum, his watchfulness and approachability. Watson is an alpha male. He has been to war, he knows how to kill someone, he is very intelligent and, if it wasn't for Holmes, he'd be the most intelligent and impressive person in the room. There is a strength to Watson and, unlike Holmes, he doesn't need to show it off. He's an understated character.

'I see very little of his performance from *The Office* in

Sherlock,' said *Sherlock* producer Sue Vertue to *The Guardian*'s John Plunkett about Freeman as Watson. 'He is just the most incredible actor. Sometimes he will say, you know this line here, I think I can do that with a look. The writers, knowing what acting chops both these boys have, have given them lines they know they are going to have fun with.'

The first episode of *Sherlock*, 'A Study In Pink', was broadcast on 25 July 2010 to great critical acclaim and high ratings, with series two broadcast in 2012 and a more successful third series in 2014. 'A Study In Pink' is a retelling of the first Holmes story, 'A Study In Scarlet', which has been recreated over seventy times. Freeman and Cumberbatch read the story because they had to bring what is unique and appealing about it into a modern context and, as such, they had to understand the characters. Episode two, which was broadcast on 1 August, is 'The Blind Banker' and episode three, 'The Great Crime', was broadcast on 8 August.

The series averaged around seven million viewers and won over the telly pundits. 'It's the best British thing that's been on telly in ages,' Freeman glowed to the *Daily Telegraph*'s Olly Grant. 'Quality will out, if that doesn't sound too arrogant. But why should I sound arrogant? I didn't write it. I just think it was undeniably good.'

The *Observer*'s critic Victoria Thorpe said, 'Freeman's dependable, capable Watson unlocks this modern Holmes, a man who now describes himself as "a high-functioning sociopath".'

'Mr. Freeman's deft performance as the grouchy but loyal Watson is one of the show's pleasures, along with Rupert

Graves's avuncular take on Inspector Lestrade,' wrote Mike Hale of the *New York Times*.

USA Today's Robert Bianco enthused, 'Cumberbatch turns *Sherlock* into an adorably aggravating blend of *House*, *The Mentalist* and Sheldon from *Big Bang* – while making him completely, compellingly his own. He's aided by an equally terrific performance by Martin Freeman (the original *Office*) as a Dr. John Watson who is no match for Holmes' intellect but is much his superior in social sense.'

Freeman won a BAFTA award for Best Supporting Actor in 2011. He was genuinely thrilled to win the award and to get such acknowledgment for his performance but he was also humble about it, knowing that it wouldn't change anything. He did not develop an ego and suddenly think he was God's gift to acting. He accepted it and moved on to his next projects.

'I'd love to think that meant that people now take me seriously in a different way,' he confessed to *Digital Spy*'s Morgan Jeffery, 'but I don't think it necessarily does. I just think it meant I was good in this show. But it's still supportive. Best actor in a bumbling role!'

Sherlock became one of the BBC's most successful contemporary dramas with a global fan base. It made both leading stars household names. The great thing about *Sherlock* is the interplay between Cumberbatch and Freeman, which is a delight to watch. They are absolutely brilliant together. It was a simple case of perfect casting. No one else could have been seen in either role. *Sherlock* has been sold to 200 countries and a US version was made called *Elementary*, with Johnny Lee Miller as Holmes and Lucy Liu as Joan Watson.

'Actually, I think it's partially financial, and partially it's cultural,' Freeman explained to *IGN Filmforce*'s Ken P. as to why American series's have more episodes than British ones. A case in point being the twenty-four-episode series of *Elementary*, now in its third season. 'I just don't think we work on that size canvas, really. And I think a lot of the time it's the differences between the writing processes. I mean, a lot of British writers don't like writing with other people – in the way that that's the lifeblood of the Americans. The really, really best stuff – the best American stuff – is never just written by one person all the time, you know?'

Martin was glad that he had finally shaken off the role of Tim Canterbury from *The Office*. He is very proud of the series and he has never complained about it; it brought him acclaim and success for something he loves doing but he is pleased to have moved on and that audiences have moved on with him.

There was an instant online reaction to *Sherlock* where fans created websites, message boards and forums dedicated to the series. *Sherlock*'s fan base is a very vocal and dedicated one.

'I don't think any one of us could have dreamt that there would be that sort of reaction,' Freeman said to the BBC. 'Never mind online, but the entirety of the success that it has had we could never have dreamt about. People used to ask me about *The Office*. They would say, "Did you know it would be this huge thing?" and there was certainly no way we could of known how big *Sherlock* could have been. I would have settled for it being a really good show that some people really loved. But the fact that it has been feted and honoured – we could never have spotted that coming.'

The lasting success of the new series is also down to the characters themselves created by Sir Arthur Conan Doyle. Sherlock Holmes has been reinvented and re-imagined countless times in the cinema, TV and even comics and, of course, literature. He is one of the most famous fictional creations of all time. The original stories are also fantastically good reads with taut plots and engaging scenarios and surprise endings. The latest update is a superbly acted, directed and written series with some beautiful designs.

What is it that makes Holmes so alluring? Why does Watson keep going back to him?

'He's a pretty magnetic bloke. He's very intelligent and there is something mesmeric about his obsessiveness as well. He's the cleverest bloke that John has ever met and he likes that challenge and the share of the danger as well. Because John is ultimately into danger as well, he is a soldier and a doctor so he is around situations that are perilous and a bit tasty, so he responds to that in Sherlock and he just wants to be around him – I sometimes don't even know why!'

Freeman had a busy schedule, but the release of a film is often dictated by the market. A small film will often sink if it is released in the summer, for example, because of its competition with Hollywood blockbusters. Thus, a film could be made one month before another film but only get a release six months later. It's the nature of the industry: some films take months – or even years – to get made; others less so.

'It honestly doesn't feel like an increased workload as I've always worked a lot,' Freeman admitted to the *University Observer*'s Steven Balbirnie. 'I mean when I was twenty-three, twenty-four I worked a lot, but obviously not in things that were ever famous. At the moment I'm lucky enough to have *Sherlock* and *The Hobbit* going on, and to have those things sort of dually going on, that's a big gig, that's a great combination.'

2010 also saw the release of *Wild Target*, on 18 June, a film which saw Freeman star as Dixon. Directed by Jonathan Lynn of *My Cousin Vinny* and *The Whole Nine Yards* fame, *Wild Target* is a loose remake of the French film from 1993, *Cible émouvante*. Filming began in September 2008 in London and the Isle Of Man and stars Bill Nighy as Victor Maynard, a middle-aged hit man who is hired by Rupert Everett's character, Ferguson, to kill Rose (Emily Blunt) after she cons Ferguson out of £900,000. Freeman's character is a sadistic assassin who is Maynard's henchman. However, the story takes a turn when Ferguson asks Dixon to dispose of Maynard, the greatest hit man ever known. The film opened in June in the UK and was met with mixed reviews. It was a box-office failure and, with a budget of £5 million, it grossed half of its budget in box office takings.

The New York Times's A.O. Scott said, 'The body count is high, but the murders are presented with neither the slapstick of a Blake Edwards *Pink Panther* caper nor the grisly shock of Quentin Tarantino pastiche. Acts of violence occur like punchlines to familiar jokes, bringing tedium rather than surprise.'

Simon Crook wrote in *Empire*, 'Lumbered with tame action and carbon-dated gags (honestly, have dead parrots been funny since *Monty Python*?), the cast just about charm their way out of it. Nighy's value, but it's a bit like watching an ITV sitcom spin-off of *A Fish Called Wanda*.'

Time Out's David Jenkins was unenthused: 'The actors do the best with what they're given – it's just a shame they've been given so little. The script is free of either zingers or insight, the inertia of the story is constantly stalled by deviation (including a superfluous homoerotic vignette which appears to be a cheap excuse to show Grint in the nude) and entire characters – including the "baddie" of the piece, Rupert Everett – are left to fade into the background.'

Freeman's career veered back to the theatre, which is in many ways his natural habitat, between 26 August and 2 October 2010, when he starred in the Royal Court theatre production of *Clybourne Park*, written by Bruce Norris (*The Pain and the Itch*) and directed by Dominic Cooke (*Aunt Dan and Lemon*, *The Fever*, *Seven Jewish Children*, *Wig Out!*, *Now Or Later* and *The Pain and the Itch*).

Freeman adopted a Chicago accent for the role. 'It was just so well-written,' he elaborated to *The Guardian*'s Euan Ferguson at the time. 'I started to read it not necessarily expecting to think of doing it – it's a while out of your life, and most things I don't want to do – but, within pages, such wit, and a real nice nastiness to it. It's also got people of different colours, different classes, echoing things that were said by people 50 years before but about a different colour or sex or power or class – it shows how things shift, and it's magnificent. It's about prejudice – literally, to prejudge a situation.'

The story tackles racism, politics and property and is set in the 1950s in contemporary America. Russ and Bev sell their two-bedroom house at a desirable, affordable price to the neighbourhood's first black family. This creates discontent amongst the white urbanities of Chicago's Clybourne Park. In 2009 the same house is up for sale and is bought by white couple Lindsey and Steve, who face a similar response from the locals in a mostly black area.

The production received rave reviews. Georgina Brown wrote in the *Mail On Sunday*, 'Dominic Cooke's flawlessly performed production culminates in a contest between Freeman's slick, white, liberal man and the super-cool, glamorous Lena (Lorna Brown, who had played the maid) to prove their total absence of prejudice by cracking the most offensively racist, sexist jokes imaginable, which, of course, only succeeds in proving the reverse. Outrageously, shockingly entertaining.'

Caroline McGinn wrote in *Time Out*, 'Above all, "Clybourne Park" makes racism personal: one reason why it walks the notoriously hard line between funny and offensive. Also, a touch of tragedy exalts and humanises the hilariously awful property rows.'

Sarah Hemming enthused in the *Financial Times*, 'The same cast play similar types in both acts and the performances would be hard to better. Martin Freeman, in particular, excels twice as the decent face of uptight white resentment, with Sarah Goldberg as his horrified wife. Provocative, troubling comedy.'

The Times's Libby Purves described Freeman as 'pleasingly unrecognisable as a terrible prat in a sports jacket'.

He also played a character named Clive Buckle in the short film *The Girl is Mime*, which, with an estimated production cost of £2,000, was released on 12 March 2011. Freeman's character is questioned by the police over the murder of his wife. Buckle says he didn't do it but the police are convinced he is the murderer – they just haven't got any evidence to prove it.

Martin then cropped up as Alvin Finkel in the film *Swinging with the Finkels*, released on 17 June 2011 in the UK and on 26 August in the States. Written and directed by Jonathan Newman, the film is about a couple – Alvin and Ellie, played by Freeman and Mandy Moore – who decide to shake up their marriage by 'swinging' with another couple. The film is part of a sub-genre of films known as 'sex comedy'. It's as British as tea, beans on toast and Cadbury's chocolate. These types of comedies go back to the 1960s and 1970s with the *Carry On* films that involve double-entendres, naughty one-liners and slapstick comedy. The early 2000s produced a few other risible films of this sort – notably, *Sex Lives of the Potato Men*, *Lesbian Vampire Killers* and *Three and Out*.

The film was poorly received. It was one of those silly British comedies that failed to hit the right buttons and engage with audiences.

Time Out's Tim Huddleston said, 'From the opening shot of Martin Freeman wandering through Borough Market to the strains of some tedious sub-Richard Curtis soul-lite, we're squarely in unambitious British romcom territory. But it's still remarkable how lazy and lacklustre *Swinging with the Finkels* manages to be.'

Total Film's Emma Didbin said, 'Thank God for Freeman, a reliably wry, likeable and emotionally truthful totem around which the rest of proceedings messily revolve. But he's saddled with a script that descends from misjudged raunch-com into mawkish sap come act three.'

Gabe Toro put the boot in with an extensive review on *IndieWire.com*: 'There's no way around this, there's no kind way to preface this, there's no purpose to side-step it: *Swinging with the Finkels* is one of the worst, cheapest, dumbest and most dishonest films of the year. The film has the same tin-ear for its material that student films usually sport, often when they're about retirement, hit men, or a litany of subjects young people tackle despite clearly having no experience in the field. "Swinging," in theory, would be a film oblivious to the matters of sex and intimacy, but, in fact, it's merely alien to any and all human behaviour.'

In 2011 Freeman took part in a charity cricket match to raise money for victims of the 2011 Christchurch earthquake. He also played Simon in *What's Your Number?* based on the book *20 Times a Lady* by Karyn Bosnak. *What's Your Number?* was a box office and critical failure after its 30 September 2011 release. It stars Ann Faris as a twenty-something woman who looks back at the men in her life and wonders if one of them was her true love.

The *Daily Telegraph*'s Tim Robey wrote, 'Faris, who has deserved exactly this lead role since her 2008 cult hit *The House Bunny*, proves once again that she has the bubblegum likeability and comic chops of peak Goldie Hawn. There are sequences here that deserve a round of applause – particularly when she tries to impress an ex (Martin Freeman) by posing as a Brit, strangled accent sliding from Eliza Doolittle to (somehow) Borat. She plays someone called Ally Darling and pulls it off, which is fairly impressive in itself.'

A.V. Club's Nathan Rabin wrote, 'There's a smart, funny,

observant comedy-drama to be made about the role our romantic pasts play in determining our futures, but director Mark Mylod and screenwriters Jennifer Crittenden (a Simpsons veteran who really should know better) and Gabrielle Allan are less interested in making that movie than in cycling Faris through a series of non-starting encounters with one-note-joke ex-flings, like the terminally British Martin Freeman or closeted gay Republican Anthony Mackie.'

Total Film's Ellen E. Jones said, 'Martin Freeman's friendly face pops up as her charming English ex, but doesn't get to do much, instead flanking Faris while she performs a bad British accent tour de force that provides the film's largest laugh.'

Freeman continued to remain dubious about Hollywood. He's never seen himself as an actor sitting by a pool in LA with a cocktail in one hand and his mobile phone in the other as he chats to his agent about movie deals. He has never allowed money to be the guiding force behind his career. Of course, he wants to make enough cash to have a comfortable life and to support his family but he's never picked a role specifically for the aid of his bank account.

'I certainly wouldn't be stupid enough to say that I wouldn't do anything Hollywoody,' he said to Olly Grant of the *Daily Telegraph*. 'It's just that I'm more of an Englishman, really, than a Hollywood man.'

What matters to Freeman is the story and the characters, whether it is a funny production or an emotional one. Everyone has been affected by a film, especially in childhood, and it's those films that have longevity.

'I'm not in a hurry to go to Hollywood, because there are

so many British actors who go "Hollywood! Hollywood! Hollywood!" and they end up doing jack-shit there. Or just nonsense. And not doing their best stuff,' he admitted to *IGN Filmforce*'s Ken P. 'But Christ, if a good director and good people wanted to work with me, I'd be over the moon! Of course, I'd sweep the floor on *The Sopranos*. But as for the idea of equating Hollywood or America with success, I find it quite abhorrent.'

He has a modest outlook on fame and his priorities are his family, his home and his health. He enjoys his life the way it is.

'There are still plenty of people who don't know who I am,' he told Steven Balbirnie of the *University Observer*. 'That hasn't changed in that way, really. It's not like everywhere I go I'm mobbed, you know, certainly not in non-English speaking places… I think your world changes as much as you want it to change. I think if you go out there and court everything, it depends on how much you embrace, how much you want it and there are some things I don't particularly want. I want work and I want to be doing good work but I don't necessarily need everything that goes with it.'

Freeman is not overly ambitious, as some actors are, but, then again, he's never been out of work. If he does not like a script, he will not audition for it but he also likes to know why actors have turned down the roles he has been offered. He is interested in good projects, regardless of nationality.

Acting is his main passion in life outside of his family and it's something he is getting better at with every passing day. His lifelong ambition is to simply refine and progress in his profession; to be a great thespian. He has little interest in much else.

He spoke to *BBC Movies*' Rob Carnevale about the possibility of one day directing a feature film: 'I'm not sure that I could. I don't know that I'd be great at that. I think the only directing I'd be any good at is theatre directing. It's the only thing I can see myself doing. But I don't feel confident enough delegating that much work on a film set. There are still things technically about films that I think are a mystery to me and I want to remain a mystery. I don't particularly want to know what everyone's job is because I've got lines to learn.'

Fame had certainly not gone to his head. He wasn't a household name – well, perhaps in Britain to a certain extent, but certainly not in America. He didn't crave Hollywood success early in his career. He doesn't really crave Hollywood success in 2015. He loves London. He always has. He's a home bird.

'It would be easy to get carried away thinking how big you are, but I'm sure the vast majority of people don't even know who I am – I'm not Robbie Williams,' he admitted to journalist Siobhan Synnot of *Douban.com*. 'Even though people come up to me in the street and say things, they still don't know my name. In America they come up to me and say, "You were in my favourite film." And it turns out their favourite film is *Love Actually*. Or *Ali G*. And they tend to assume I have been unemployed since then. So I'm not about to be Tom Cruise.'

He never went knocking on Hollywood's door. He didn't need to because Hollywood called him, or rather New Zealand did.

CHAPTER SEVEN

THE HOBBIT IN NEW ZEALAND

'When people call me an everyman they think it's a
compliment. I want to rip their fucking eyeballs out. I don't
want to be the cosiest man in Britain; it's not the way I feel
about the world or the job I do.'
FREEMAN SPEAKING TO BRUCE DESSAU IN THE
LONDON EVENING STANDARD, 2005

2012 would bring some incredible opportunities to Freeman as he returned to Baker Street and also made a trip to Middle Earth in the great fantasy world of author J.R.R. Tolkien.

The writers of *Sherlock*, Mark Gatiss and Steven Moffat, came to the conclusion that they should rework three of Conan Doyle's most well-known stories as the friendship between Holmes and Watson developed. Even Watson was brought in as the lead detective in episode two, 'The Hounds Of Baskerville', which was sandwiched between 'A Scandal In Belgravia' (aired 1 January 2012) and 'The Reichenbach Fall' (aired 15 January 2012) and was first shown on TV on 8 January 2012.

The series-two finale, 'The Reichenbach Fall', was Freeman's favourite episode to film. He was very excited about it as soon as he'd read the script. The finished programme is superlative.

The Washington Post's Hank Stuever said of Cumberbatch

and Freeman, 'He's [Cumberbatch] quite something, all right, but I can't be the only one who finds this particular version of *Sherlock* to be a little grating. He'd be almost unwatchable if it weren't for the tender devotion and counterbalance Martin Freeman brings to the role of Watson.'

Den of Geek's Louisa Mellor wrote, 'Cumberbatch and Freeman remain a fantastic double act, with even more bickering and gags at their status as a couple this time around. There can't be a greater pleasure on telly at the moment than seeing the look of arch disdain on Cumberbatch's face dissolve into boyish giggles with Freeman on a sofa in Buckingham Palace, or in the back of a cab.'

As with any friendship, partnership or marriage, there is a familiarity between the pair and, as such, there is also contempt and love, compassion and everything else that is fuelled in a relationship. They've settled for each other. The relationship between Holmes and Watson is what the public have enjoyed about the series. It was a gratifying experience for both Freeman and Cumberbatch to see how much the characterisation between the two characters had progressed. The writing is excellent and, when the scripts are so good, that's half the job done.

The duo may be best friends on screen but behind the camera, due to their busy schedules, they don't have the closeness of Holmes and Watson.

'We are very friendly [Benedict and I] and we're good work colleagues but we're also quite busy and I don't really hang out with many of, or any of, my co-stars,' Freeman admitted to *Yahoo*.

There's a tendency for the public to think that actors hang out with each other and become lifelong friends after a film is made, which may be true in some cases but, for the most part, actors work together on set for a few weeks or months and, through the nature of the job, they automatically make friends but once filming is wrapped up they move on and perhaps never see each other again.

Freeman added, 'It's obviously because of the closeness of that relationship on screen, people expect it, or want it to be echoed in real life, which is understandable… You want all your favourite band members to live together in a flat and they don't.'

Martin spoke to *ShortList.com* about the show's increasingly rapid and ever-growing fan base: '… *Sherlock* is a much finer line between love and hate [laughs]. Because they love it so much that they have to hate it as well and they have to sort of hate you, or hate aspects of what you do, or hate Stephen [sic] Moffat if he's said something that is half a degree off menu for what they want him to say.'

It's fun to watch the relationship between Holmes and Watson develop throughout the first two series. It has become more of a partnership with Watson only one step behind Holmes rather than six. Watson still gets annoyed by some aspects of Holmes's behaviour but he learns how to deal with the detective's quirky and eccentric personality. Even with the nail-biting scenes between Holmes and Moriarty, Watson still has a presence there. The writers have not side-lined him at all. Moriarty is one of the most famous villains in all of literature and he comes across remarkably well in the series.

At the same time that *Sherlock* series two was broadcast director Guy Ritchie released the sequel, *A Game of Shadows*, to his surprise blockbuster Hollywood version of Sherlock Holmes with the American Robert Downey Jr as Holmes and Brit actor Jude Law as Watson.

'Well, obviously Jude has the misfortune of not being very good-looking, so he has to watch jealously,' Freeman joked with *Empire*'s Nick de Semlyen. 'No, we all went to see the first film and came away going, "We wanted to hate that, but we didn't." It was very entertaining and I love Jude. He's good.'

'A Scandal In Belgravia' was nominated for thirteen Primetime Emmy Awards, including 'Outstanding Supporting Actor In A Miniseries Or Movie' for Freeman's portrayal of Watson, while Freeman bagged the TV Movie/Miniseries Supporting Actor award at the Gold Derby TV Awards in May 2012. The episode won three British Academy Television Craft Awards and later the Edgar Award for 'Best Episode In A TV Series' in May 2013.

'It's a very good idea not to read reviews, because for better or for worse, you can end up "playing the review". But I have [read them] – that's why I'm awful in the second series!' he said to *Digital Spy*'s Morgan Jeffery in 2011. 'I didn't actively seek [reviews] out, but we've all got an ego and if you know people are saying really nice things about you, you tend to open your ears. But I wasn't maniacal about hunting down everything, because most actors hunt down the bad stuff – you want to know who thinks you're a prick!'

Sherlock was inundated with further awards and nominations in 2012. Freeman picked up a Tumblr TV Award for Outstanding Supporting Actor In A Drama Series, a Crime Thriller Award for Best Supporting Actor and a nomination at the PAAFTJ Awards for Best Supporting Actor In A Miniseries Or TV Movie. The series won a PAAFTJ Award for Best Cast In A Miniseries or TV Movie and Best Cast at the Tumblr TV Awards.

Freeman continued to be shocked by the success of the series.

'Some of the viewing figures we got with the second series of *Sherlock* were fucking outrageous,' he told *Esquire*'s Michael Holden in 2012. 'One week we beat *EastEnders*, and I'm so proud – not because we beat *EastEnders* – but I'm just proud that millions, I mean literally millions and millions, of people wanted to watch it then. That night, do you know what I mean?'

Aside from *Sherlock*, Freeman voiced the character of 'The Pirate with a Scarf' in the 2012 film, *The Pirates! In an Adventure with Scientists!* which was renamed in New Zealand as *The Pirates! Band of Misfits*. Directed by Peter Lord, *The Pirates! In an Adventure with Scientists!* is a British-American 3D stop-motion film produced by Aardman Animations, the British company behind *Chicken Run* and *Wallace and Gromit*.

Freeman had wanted to work with Nick Park and his Bristol-based Aardman Animations for a while and had first approached Park about a possible collaboration at a British Comedy Awards several years earlier.

Hugh Grant made his first animated feature debut while Imelda Staunton, David Tennant, Jeremy Piven, Salma Hayek, Lenny Henry and Brian Blessed also lent their voices to the film. It is loosely based on the book of the same name in the Gideon Defoe *The Pirates!* series.

Freeman told a journalist at *Douban.com* about his experience with voice work, which is everything Martin doesn't want acting to be – alone in a room reading from a script.

'It was very unique, you don't even know what their physicality is,' he said. 'I had seen minutes here and there of what my character was going to be, I knew what he was going to look like, but he's not literally me. I was doing the physicality that you normally are in an acting job, but you leave his actual physicality to the team of animators, a team of people you hadn't met in another city somewhere. There's a lot of trust, I suppose, that goes on – definitely on both sides. I think from our point of view you feel quite privileged to be on the film anyway, every actor who was in it was, I'm sure, was quite chuffed to be a part of it, having seen all their work previously.'

Freeman much prefers to work with actors and, while it was a new experience for him, he was genuinely only interested because it was an opportunity to work with Aardman. He didn't get into acting to do this sort of work though because, for the most part, voice work is working alone. Freeman loves people and being sociable and voice work does not provide that sort of interaction. Acting is more 'community based', as he has described it. He loves to hear stories on set from other actors and mingle with the cast and crew.

Martin's inspiration for his character, Pirate With Scarf, was John Le Mesurier in *Dad's Army*; basically someone who is cleverer than his superior and is level headed and knows how to deal with his superior officer. Freeman's character is the

Captain's right-hand man. His Captain takes him for granted sometimes but knows he can rely on him. Pirate With Scarf would run through hoops for his Captain. In the film Pirate Captain gets a crisis of confidence and forgets how much high esteem his crew hold him in so, when he starts to feel negatively about himself, Pirate With Scarf boost up his boss's confidence. None of the characters in the film have names as such – Pirate With Scarf, Curvaceous Pirate, Pirate With Gout and so on – and so they're more like stock characters.

It was a reasonable box-office success after its 28 March release but it was a critical hit and was nominated for the 2013 Academy Award for Best Animated Feature.

Time's Richard Corliss wrote, '*The Pirates!*, for all its vagrant appeal, isn't in that exalted category; it lacks urgency and coherence. The movie is like a pirate without a parrot, Darwin without Natural Selection, Wallace without Gromit.'

LA Times's Kenneth Turan enthused, 'The twists and turns of the *Pirates* plot are many, but hanging on for the duration is a pleasure. The visual treats are many, including random signage ("Live Sports: Urchin Throwing, Cockney Baiting" reads one) and a clever riff on movie maps that illustrate nautical progress.'

The New York Times reported it was: 'More eccentric than whimsical, *Band of Misfits* is set in a somewhat louder, rowdier key than some of Aardman's earlier charmers. It's the first of the studio's stop-motion features to be shot in digital and the first shot in 3-D, developments that some Aardman purists may find the outrageous equivalent of Bob Dylan going electric or David Fincher going digital.'

A short film was also released on 13 August called *So You*

Want To Be A Pirate! which features the voices of Freeman, Hugh Grant, Brian Blessed, David Tennant and Russell Tovey.

Freeman also had a part in an almost forgotten half-English, half-Spanish fantasy film called *Animals*, co-written and directed by Marçal Forés, best known for his work on a BBC pilot ('The Things I Haven't Told You') that never became a series. The film is about a teenager named Pol who lives with his brother and is still at school. He has a fairly ordinary life but he has a secret – his cuddly teddy bear, Deerhoof, can think, talk and move. Pol shares his secrets with him. The school that he attends sees the arrival of a student called Ikari, who is an elusive somewhat enigmatic character with something to hide. Pol is intrigued by Ikari and his interest in his new classmate sparks off a series of dark and disturbing events that turn his life from the ordinary into the extraordinary. It was released in Spain on 22 October 2012.

The Hollywood Reporter's Neil Young wrote of the film, 'A self-satisfied slice of quirky Catalan cool, *Animals* boasts flashes of brilliance but squanders considerable potential on a waywardly sophomoric script. Sales prospects for the slick-looking feature debut of Barcelona's Marçal Forés are boosted by a photogenic young cast, the large amount of English-language dialogue and the unexpected presence in a supporting role of popular British star Martin Freeman – Bilbo Baggins in the upcoming *Hobbit* trilogy. But while combining *Ted* and *Donnie Darko* – with touches of *Afterschool* and *Ghost World* – sounds like a promising concept on paper, the results are too strenuously weird for anything other than marginal youth interest.'

Variety's Jonathan Holland wrote, 'Troubled teens and a

talking teddy bear populate the bizarre world of *Animals*, Catalan helmer Marçal Forés' shimmering, ambitious debut. This stylishly wrought item shuttles between fantasy and realism a la *Donnie Darko* in its exploration of its protag's problematic emotional life, although too much of the lead character's delicate, self-regarding preciousness spills over into the film itself. But while the last half-hour has an anything-goes air, there's still enough verve and quality in the early reels – including some wonderfully dreamy atmospherics – to suggest that Forés is one to watch. Limited fest pickups are likely.'

Freeman's role in the film came as a surprise to many fans and to this day it remains something of an oddity in his arsenal of movies.

DVD Talk's Tyler Foster wrote of the DVD release, '*Animals* is a frustrating film, packed to the brim with symbolism that director Marçal Forés has trouble stringing into a cohesive story. Watching the trailer, the film looks like a bizarre dark fantasy which has no boundaries, pitching Pol's emotional growth as the start of a rift between himself and the bear that turns bloody, but the actual movie is far more contained, trying to string together important bits of subtext into a portrait of teen angst. At times, the film touches on feelings that young people, especially gay teens, may find incredibly familiar, but Forés complicates his movie with too many subplots and additional ideas to explore, resulting in a murk that prevents the film from having much of a point.'

Does Freeman have an agenda when it comes to choosing roles? What inspires him as an actor?

'It has to be something of interest to me, and I have to be able to bring something that interests me,' he said to the *Sunday Times*'s Benji Wilson. 'There has to be a story and a three dimensional aspect to the character.'

There's always a chance of win or lose with every project. As with any freelance endeavour, the chances of success can be fifty-fifty.

He spoke to *Nerd Repository*'s Kyle Wilson about the gamble that is acting full-time: 'I think you just have to take a leap of faith as so many things are in life and so many jobs are a leap of faith because you're not seeing the finished result. You can't come in at the end and go, I knew *The Godfather* was going to X, Y and Z. On the way to making *The Godfather*, of course, it could have been many other things. It's all a big leap of faith.'

Freeman ventured into another left-field project with a Radio 3 adaptation of B.S. Johnson's 1960s 'experimental' novel, *The Unfortunates*. The author, now barely remembered, killed himself aged forty in 1973 as he struggled to gain commercial success. *The Unfortunates* was written in a stream of consciousness and published in 1969. Martin plays a sports writer who is sent to a city on an assignment but is soon faced with the ghosts of his past, notably that of a friend who tragically died of cancer. The character is something of an everyman, so it was perfect casting for Freeman, despite his reluctance to play such a part. The production edit saw the recording divided into eighteen sections and randomised before the broadcast and then placed on a 'carousel' on the Radio 3 website so listeners could choose at random.

'I just thought it was an interesting idea,' Freeman said to

Left: Martin Freeman's first big break came in the celebrated TV show *The Office*. The cast (*from left*: Ricky Gervais, Ash Atalla, Martin Freeman, Lucy Davis and Stephen Merchant) were together at the 61st Golden Globes to collect the award for Best Series.

Right: The London premiere of *The Hitchhikers Guide to the Galaxy* was a happy event for the stars Freeman, Zooey Deschanel and Sam Rockwell.

Freeman has always been protective over the private life he shares with his better half, actress Amanda Abbington. However, they enjoyed a very public 'wedding' when they appeared together in Sherlock in 2013.

Above: *Fargo* aired in 2014 to great acclaim and an Emmy for Outstanding Miniseries with Freeman appearing with a strong Minnesotan accent in the lead role of Lester Nygaard.

Below: The role of a lifetime: being cast as Bilbo Baggins changed Freeman's life. The cast of the final *Hobbit* film gathered in London on 1 December 2014 for the premiere; Freeman's journey to Middle Earth had finally come to an end.

Above left: Filming *Sherlock* at Gloucester Cathedral in early 2015 – with a fairly prominent moustache.

Above right: As comfortable on the stage as in front of the cameras, Freeman appeared as the malformed King Richard in *Richard III*, directed by Jamie Lloyd.

Below: Possibly his best-loved role, Freeman and Cumberbatch form an incredible partnership in *Sherlock*.

All photos © Rex Features

the *Daily Telegraph*'s Olly Grant. 'I hadn't heard of the book before. Or of B.S. Johnson. But I liked the idea of a book being published in no particular order, and of applying that to a radio version.'

The book's shapelessness has been played up in an intriguing way.

'They did it like an FA Cup draw,' he explains. 'They put the chapters on little wooden balls and then drew them out [one by one] to get a random result.'

Rachel Cooke wrote in *The Guardian*, 'Although I'm always slightly confused by the concept of drama on Radio 3 (I mean, why?), I enjoyed listening to it. Freeman was just right; his bewildered mildness captured perfectly the tone of the book, which is sometimes comic, sometimes elusive, and occasionally very affecting.'

The big news of 2012 was that Freeman had been cast as Bilbo Baggins, the lead character, in *The Hobbit: An Unexpected Journey*, which is the first one in a three-part film adaptation of the 1937 novel *The Hobbit* by the late fantasy author J.R.R. Tolkien, who created *The Lord of the Rings*. *The Hobbit* is a prequel to director Peter Jackson's *The Lord of the Rings* film trilogy.

The New Zealand director had made his name on a series of 'splatstick' (a combination of slapstick comedy and blood-and-gore) horror comedies such as *Bad Taste* and *Braindead* before moving onto such Hollywood blockbusters as *King Kong* and, obviously, *The Lord of the Rings* trilogy. His name is now in the same ranks as James Cameron and Steven Spielberg as one of the most successful film-makers of all time.

It truly hit home that Martin Freeman was cast as Bilbo Baggins when people congratulated him on the street in London. It was the first time he'd ever been recognised for a job he had not yet done. It then took months to get the make-up and attire fitted for the part. It was a gradual process of getting his feet sized up, the plaster cast made for his head and ears and so on.

The massively successful film trilogy had already grown into a billion-dollar empire; the third part, *The Return of the King*, won the Best Picture Oscar in 2003. Jackson was desperate to return to Middle Earth with much of the same cast and crew. The journey to the big screen would be a long and laborious one.

The screenplay was written by Jackson with his long-time collaborators Fran Walsh (Jackson's partner), Philippa Boyens and director Guillermo del Toro, who was originally slated to direct the film (with Jackson as producer) before quitting the project – due to delays and financial problems – in 2010 after working on the planned two-film project for two years. *The Hobbit: An Unexpected Journey* is set in Middle Earth years before the events of *The Lord of the Rings* took place. The film expands on the original book with portions adapted from the 125-page appendices and footnotes of *The Return of the King*, the third novel of *The Lord of the Rings* trilogy. The 1937 novel was originally conceived for children and offers none of the dark adventures of *The Lord of the Rings* but rather a more gentle fantasy adventure. Said footnotes and appendices were published over twenty years after the original publication of *The Hobbit* and were known only among the series's most eager aficionados.

Peter Jackson explained his reasons for including the extra angles at the 2012 Comic-Con: 'In these appendices, he did talk about what happened, and it was a lot darker and more serious than what's written in *The Hobbit*. Also, to be quite honest, I want to make a series of movies that run together, so if any crazy lunatic wants to watch them all in a row, there will be a consistency of tone. I don't want to make a purely children's story, followed by *The Lord of the Rings*. We are providing a balance. A lot of the comedy and the charm and the fairy tale quality of *The Hobbit* comes from the characters.'

It was during this time that series two of *Sherlock* was being filmed. The schedules of both Freeman and Cumberbatch proved difficult for the writers and even Moffat (the head writer of *Doctor Who*) and Gatiss were very busy themselves.

'Yes, it is true he nearly turned down *The Hobbit* because he was already committed to the second series of *Sherlock*,' said actor Amanda Abbington, his long-term partner of twelve years, in an article by Cheryl Stonehouse of the *Daily Express*. 'Martin is never fazed by anything. He's never star-struck. He's a very talented man but he never forgets where real life is. A commitment is a commitment.'

Freeman is very loyal to *Sherlock*. He didn't want to turn down *The Hobbit* and he could have left *Sherlock* but he didn't want to because he loves the series and is very proud of it.

'... the BBC weren't making it particularly easy for me to negotiate,' he admitted to the *Sunday Times*'s Benji Wilson. 'They weren't going, "Yeah, fine." They were going, "No. We wanna do this, we wanna do it now." I remember the conversation with my agent, and I was saying, "Are we going to have to let *The Hobbit* go?" and he went, "Yeah, I think we are.'"

The delays in production and the financial issues that had delayed *The Hobbit* seemed to work in Freeman's favour, though by the time the film was given the official green light, Freeman had signed on for the second series of *Sherlock*. It was on, off, on again and off because it seemed like it would clash with shooting *Sherlock*. Martin was enormously disappointed, as was Jackson.

'I met Peter in England and spent the afternoon with him while the World Cup was on,' Freeman explained to *UK Ask Men*'s Jamie Watt. 'He was about as normal as you can be, and I appreciated the fact that he understood my misgivings about being away from home for so long. I really wanted to do the film, and when it looked like I had to walk away from the role because of *Sherlock*, that wasn't a very amusing scenario. But, you know, these things happen and I put that behind me and I just hoped that I was going to hate it when it came out.'

Six weeks away from the shoot, Jackson still hadn't signed anyone; he was thinking of other actors but Freeman was his main choice. He was stressed and having sleepless nights. An avid *Sherlock* fan, Peter Jackson was so keen to cast Freeman as Bilbo Baggins that he fitted the film's production around the actor's schedule.

'Martin was the only person that we wanted for that role, and that was really before we met Martin,' Jackson told reporters at a press event in New York. 'We knew him from [the BBC's] *The Office* and *Hitchhiker's Guide* [*to the Galaxy*], and we just felt he had qualities that would be perfect for Bilbo. The stuffy, repressed English quality. He's a dramatic actor, he's not a comedian, but he has a talent for comedy.'

If Jackson didn't have enough clout in Hollywood, the studio would never have accepted the change in schedule because Freeman was not a big enough name yet. But Jackson and his creative team were adamant that Martin was the man for the role.

'Peter moved heaven and earth for me so when I got to New Zealand to begin filming I felt very welcome and loved,' said Freeman to the *Daily Telegraph*'s John Hiscock. 'It was a huge compliment to me, but I think there are plenty of other actors who could have given Bilbo a go – I'm not the only one.'

Ships like this don't sail very often and Freeman, at this stage in his career, was willing to move away from his family for a short while for the chance of progressing his career. He was truly gutted when he thought he had to turn the part down.

Martin was aware of the extensive online campaign to get him the part in the first place. It was humbling if slightly odd.

'I have enough faith in Peter to know,' he told *Dark Horizons*' Garth Franklin. 'I know that he's… 'Cause he's said to me about other things he's done, where he's taken maybe too much notice of what was happening on the Internet, and actually been given a bum steer. I think he's learned from that. We can all look at the Internet and go, "He hates me! Oh, but she loves me. Oh, but he hates me…" you know. That way, madness lies. So I think yeah, it's very nice, it's gratifying that people wanted me to be in it. But they didn't get me the job.'

What was it about Freeman that made Jackson so passionate that he was a perfect fit for the part?

'I think he saw a strange looking bloke with an odd face,' Freeman joked to *Hampshire Life*'s Frank Grice. 'Quite a small, round face and someone who would fit the ears. Honestly, I genuinely don't know. I'm not being cute with that answer; I don't know what he saw. Hopefully, he thinks I'm quite good, and so could do it, I hope.'

He added, 'I think, sometimes, you got to be careful what you wish for. Of course we all want to be told we're brilliant in various ways. And then, if someone thinks were brilliant for a reason we find unflattering, then we'd rather not hear it.'

The problem of schedule conflicts was solved. Jackson flew Freeman to New Zealand for four months on *The Hobbit* before sending him back to England for two months on *Sherlock*. It meant that the director spent longer on editing and was able to make adjustments to the film, which he would not have been able to do otherwise. Jackson called Freeman, who at the time was rehearsing in London, to tell him the film was back on. Martin was enormously flattered that Jackson had gone to so much effort.

'To be fair, *Sherlock* wasn't really budging, the BBC weren't really budging so Peter Jackson budged and rearranged the entire shooting schedule of *The Hobbit* so I could do both. Which is very flattering and very lucky for me,' Freeman explained to the *University Observer*'s Steven Balbirnie. 'So it meant that I could film some of *The Hobbit* and have downtime to go and do *Sherlock* series two and come back to *The Hobbit*. It's amazing that I got to do both.'

If it wasn't for *Sherlock*, Freeman would have had to have spent eighteen months working on *The Hobbit*, which would have made time with his family rather difficult, but he and his partner, Abbie Abbington, knew that either way he could not turn it down. Freeman has worked on other films that he loves more but none of them would end up making a billion dollars at the box office. That sort of opportunity is a once-in-a-lifetime offer. Only a crank would turn it down.

'His heart ached a little bit,' Abbington told the *Daily Mail*'s Vicky Power regarding Martin spending time away from his family. 'But we know the film is going to be huge. He does get stressed, though. Sometimes he rings me up at 7am to say, "I've been covered in crap, hanging upside down and I've got bloody ears on." But he knows it's for the greater good and he does it with a smile.'

Freeman did not get into acting because he wanted his name on billboards, movie posters and to be on TV chat shows. He chose to be an actor because of films such as the classic *Dog Day Afternoon* with Al Pacino, one of Freeman's acting heroes. It's not about the size or scale of a film, it's about the story and characters. If the size of the film is huge but the script is poor, he's not interested but, if it is a good solid script, then he's game. He'll do his best to serve the story. He's not concerned about how big he is in it but rather how good he is.

The Hobbit was a potentially huge film but with a strong script. The one thing he learned from accepting *The Hobbit* was not to be so reticent about taking on roles outside of his comfort zone.

'Being an actor is just like being any other sort of self-employed person – we're all just happy to have a job in the first place, but we also thrive off the uncertainty of it,' Freeman admitted to UK's *Ask Men*'s Jamie Watt. 'I didn't see any of my previous roles coming either. With film, there's art and then there's scale, and some people, like Peter, are able to marry the two of those together brilliantly. I honestly wouldn't give a fuck about these movies if they were just about scale, but you actually care about the characters in these films.'

When it was officially announced that Freeman had landed the part, fans were ecstatic. He was just the right actor for the job. His friend Simon Pegg, a science-fiction and fantasy nut, laughed that Freeman would have to do the gruelling convention circuit.

'Martin's the anti-me: a soul aficionado and a vinyl junkie – absolutely not a resident of the geek universe. Not the type of person who will relish the attention he'll get for being Bilbo Baggins. Ha!' Pegg told *The Observer*'s Tom Lamont.

As with *The Lord of the Rings* films, *The Hobbit* movies were produced back–to-back over an eighteen-month period with principal photography commencing on 21 March 2011 in Jackson's native New Zealand. Filming ended after 266 days on 6 July 2012. Pick-ups (minor filming to augment a scene) for *The Hobbit: An Unexpected Journey* took place in July. Freeman enjoyed the experience of filming in New Zealand and he was certainly appreciative of it but he missed his family, London, his tailor, his record collection and Bar Italia. He told *Flicks And Bits* in 2013 that 'It was lovely. I had never been to New Zealand before. It's as far you can go from London before you fall off the world [laughs]. I knew a couple of the cast loosely from London, obviously my old mate Benedict, but I didn't know anybody well at first.'

He's never lived anywhere else but Britain but now he could say he's lived in New Zealand. He didn't stay in a hotel, he lived in a house. Kiwis for the most part have a less stressful life than Brits, so there was a different way of living to accommodate to. Freeman found that the locals made it a very easy place to work. The cast and crew, mostly from the US and the UK, have generally stated how at home they were made to feel by the locals.

Aside from Cumberbatch, there were no familiar faces on set so the first day reminded him of going to a new school. A great deal of time was spent rehearsing, which Freeman humorously dubbed 'Dwarf boot camp', where he learned how to be a hobbit and the rest of the cast learned to be dwarves or some other fantastical creatures out of the pages of the Tolkien novel. Freeman bonded with Elijah Wood over a mutual love of The Beatles. They ate, drank and got to know each other like chums. By the time the cameras started rolling on the first day of the shoot, they felt comfortable with each other and friendships had begun developing.

'You find out so much in those first few days,' he told *Dark Horizon*'s Garth Franklin. 'You just come along, in a way, and be open and ready and receptive. Bring whatever you've got to bring, but don't bring too much because it's not a done deal yet. It grew as the weeks and months went on, really.'

In the story, the great wizard Gandalf the Grey (Ian McKellen) convinces Bilbo Baggins to accompany thirteen dwarves, led by Thorin Oakenshield (Richard Armitage), on a quest to reclaim the Lonely Mountain from the dragon Smaug (Benedict Cumberbatch). The cast also included Christopher Lee, Hugo

Weaving, James Nesbitt, Sylvester McCoy, Cate Blanchett, Elijah Wood, Andy Serkis, Ken Stott and Barry Humphries.

Coming from the modern-day Baker Street of *Sherlock* to the Middle Earth of *The Hobbit* was an odd experience for Freeman but an interesting one. It was a challenge but that is the nature of his job as an actor. The film charts Bilbo's journey, yet it was filmed out of order, which Freeman found difficult, so that brought more homework and training for Martin and his fellow actors.

'There are lots of things that keep me awake at night, but work isn't one of them,' Freeman admitted to *Empire* magazine's Nick de Semlyen. 'I mean, no one's going to die if someone doesn't like what I do. So I don't feel a great pressure. The first day of *The Hobbit* was nervy, but in a fun way, and with *Sherlock* obviously the success of the first series helps. At least a few people loved it, so hopefully we'll have a fair bit of goodwill for the second series. Unless we fuck it up!'

Jackson and Freeman worked well together. The actor was well aware that it was Peter Jackson's film and that he was in charge; that he knows the world of *The Hobbit* better than anyone else. But it would have been awful for Freeman to travel so far away from his family and to take on a role of that size without having any creative input and without being able to express his opinion. Jackson made enough room for Martin to get involved. There was a great deal of respect between the two men. But, of course, the director had to be pleased with everything. Freeman is the best and greatest critic of his own work though, so he was able to make his own choices as regards Bilbo. Early on in the filming process Freeman and

Jackson discussed who they thought Bilbo Baggins was and how he should come across on screen.

As with *The Hitchhiker's Guide to the Galaxy*, Freeman was far from an expert on the original novel. Fantasy just isn't his thing.

'It wasn't in my orbit at all' he told *Empire* magazine. 'I'm not sure it would have been very helpful if I'd always wanted to play Bilbo Baggins. I'd have come up against someone else's vision. We're taking the work seriously, but when we're looking up at tennis balls that are meant to be trolls, it's got to be fun.'

Freeman had never met Ian Holm, who played Bilbo in Jackson's *Lord of the Rings* trilogy, and he would have loved to but that was never the original set-up. Martin had Holm's blessing though, so that created some positivity and Freeman just had to follow his own way into the role. Ian Holm had established Bilbo Baggins as a character on screen but Freeman was conscious not to copy him just for the sake of it. Martin was cast because not only is he an excellent actor but he's also a good fit for the part. Of course, for research Freeman watched *The Lord of the Rings* films again and in more detail but he didn't study Ian Holm's performance as such. Martin knew why he had been cast and it was not because he could copy other actors, but rather because he is a self-styled thespian, perfectly capable of tackling the role. During his scenes he wasn't thinking, 'How would Ian have done this?' He was starting from scratch with his own version of the character. He didn't feel as though he had anything to live up to – he had faith in himself as an actor and the creative team evidently had faith in his abilities too.

Freeman spoke to *Collider*'s Steve 'Frosty' Weintraub about the role: 'I think if I was, I don't know, Jeff Goldblum or someone, then I might be thinking, "Right, hang on, if he's the older me, I'd better attend more to something else maybe." Well, grow, for a start. But no, 'cause I think I was always trusted with it. All I was told, which I think was flattery, and probably bollocks, was, "You are the only person to play it." So I thought, "Well, if they think that, then I've got to trust that." And there's only so much you can run with someone else's thing. It's very helpful, in the way that it's brilliant as he is always brilliant, and it's a beautiful establisher of that character, and a very loved one, for obvious reasons.'

The first day on set for Freeman was in Gollum's cave, so he got to work with performance-capture maestro Andy Serkis, which on its own was an experience-and-a-half.

He told Garth Franklin of *Dark Horizons*, 'I was working with Andy as Gollum, which in itself is interesting. Fascinating as a baptism of fire, but friendly fire because he's so good. That character is so beloved and he knows that character, obviously, as well as anybody knows anything.'

Speaking about the experience, Serkis told journalists at Comic-Con in 2012, 'We were able to shoot a scene in its entirety, on a live set, with Martin's performance being captured on a digital camera while Gollum's performance used a performance-capture camera, and captured them both, at exactly the same moment in time. What that does is that there's no disconnect. The fidelity to the moment, the choices and the beats that you create, between the director and the actors, is absolutely nailed in one. That makes a significant difference to the believability and the emotion. Therefore, the chances to augment and change the iteration on the fly makes a huge difference.'

This sort of high-scale film was not something Freeman had experienced before – even *The Hitchhikers Guide to the Galaxy* was not this gargantuan in scope. Freeman felt safe because Serkis knew the character and is an expert at what he does. The first few days on set for Martin were about finding his feet. He learned so much as he was getting to grips with everything on set. It was important for him to be receptive and open to ideas. It was a long stint so Freeman had the chance to look back and ponder if he had done things right. Usually, acting gigs don't last that long, so it was all a new experience.

Working with all the various technologies and cameras was difficult at first for Freeman, who was used to a more basic style of film-making, but *The Hobbit* was filmed for 3D and forty-eight frames per second rather than the standard twenty-four. A scene would be set up and filmed but then there'd be a technical issue with the new 'Slave-Mo-Co' camera system, which would halt filming. Freeman was not a fan of the new technological system, which was used for the Bag End scene with Gandalf and the dwarves. The breakdown of technology was especially prominent in the early days of shooting and the actors found it difficult but they persevered. The multiple takes were mostly down to technical issues. Some film-makers, such as Clint Eastwood, are known for just one or two takes before the next scene is set up; other film-makers, such as David Fincher, could do dozens of takes. Freeman's experience was mostly in independent films where time is of the essence and filming is wrapped up in six weeks. Though he is an accomplished actor and had not been out of work since leaving drama school, in this case he was still learning the tricks of the trade. What was good about the technology issues was that they got more opportunity to rehearse so, by the time the cameras were set up for another take, the actors were finely tuned.

3D is a cause of controversy and criticism among film fans. Since the release of James Cameron's 2009 science-fiction film *Avatar*, 3D has been all the rage with Hollywood film-makers. Of course, ticket prices are more expensive and studios therefore make more money but some film fans believe it to be a phase. 'I'm not particularly committal or non-committal to 3D,' Freeman admitted to Garth Franklin of *Dark Horizons*. 'I never watched *The Godfather* and went, "Do you know what this needs? This needs Fredo's hand coming out at you." I think as long as it's used tastefully, and as long as it's used to enhance something, that's fine. As soon as… the medium is the message, then no. I trust Peter. He's a pretty well-versed film-maker, and he's got pretty good taste.'

Martin did not realise how small his character and those of the dwarves were until they stood next to Gandalf. Freeman's scale double wasn't used excessively though. He got used to the ways of filming rather quickly, much to his surprise.

He told reporters at the 2012 Comic-Con, 'The first time that we ever shot a scene with Gandalf, where Ian had to be in a completely different room, I thought, "This is ridiculous! This will never work! Who are these people? Why are they doing this to us?" And then, an hour later, you go, "That looks brilliant!" You rehearse it and rehearse it, and it becomes normal. Your whole frame of reference for how you normally work on a film shifts. What, one minute, is completely unworkable and ridiculous, the next week just works. It becomes very easy, actually.'

Another new experience for Freeman was wearing prosthetics. He got off lightly as he did not have to wear a great deal of prosthetic make-up but some of his co-stars found it very tough. It can get hot and claustrophobic. Filming lasted for upwards of ten months and the cast had to wear this make-up constantly while working, so all this added a lot of stress and discomfort to the work. Who said filming was easy!

British actor Richard Armitage, who plays Thorin Oakenshield, spoke to the *Radio Times*'s Susanna Lazarus about working with Martin Freeman: 'He's just brilliant. He's so inventive and he keeps the atmosphere on set really buoyant because he's got a natural sense of comedy, as Martin but also as Bilbo Baggins. He really experiments with the role and he makes me work in a different way. He's always having a bit of a laugh but when it comes to doing the serious stuff he can always pull it out the bag.'

Freeman had never previously done such a lengthy job, so it was especially helpful that, despite the huge male cast, there were no egos or falling-outs.

The days were long and the weeks were longer so Freeman and his fellow cast members cherished their days off and used them for a bit of R&R.

Freeman said to *Stuff*'s Tom Cardy, 'It's good, it's always nice to have a day off. But I can't complain, because on this block [of filming], I've had quite a lot of days off. It's been quite nice, actually. Unexpected, but still relatively rare. Yeah, days off are always good. However much you're enjoying the job, and I am enjoying this job, it's always nice to be out and go and have some Japanese food.'

What did Freeman think of his character, the famed Bilbo Baggins?

'Bilbo went through a few faces. There were a couple of noses,' Martin said to reporters at a press conference. 'They had the idea of having a more snub nose, and then they decided that my nose was weird enough. So it went from a more middle-aged rocker to being what Bilbo looks like now, which is a middle-aged rocker. So it was gradual; it wasn't one minute you are you and then the next minute you are the character. It was incremental.'

Being a bit of a mod, Freeman even made a joke about 'Moddit', with a 'little paisley scarf, a little bit of brocade. I'm doing what I can. A wine coloured corduroy jacket...' he told *Esquire*'s Michael Holden.

The Hobbit takes a different turn from *The Lord of the Rings*. It's a much lighter, family oriented film but with dashings of darkness. The film sees Bilbo Baggins become a hero, which is ultimately the film's greatest evolution, but his heroism comes out of necessity. He comes into situations where, unless he does things, he and his friends will die. The history of fantasy cinema is littered with unlikely heroes and, of course, Bilbo Baggins is now one of the most indelible.

There was much riding on Freeman's casting and he felt a great deal of responsibility, though he realised that the ultimate job would be down to the final edit.

He explained his thoughts on his casting in the film to *Collider*'s Steve 'Frosty' Weintraub: 'In the doing of it, it's ultimately my responsibility, but then obviously the greater responsibility, of course, is Peter's, because he has his eye on the ball – well, on various different balls all the time. And also, he's got a picture in his head of how it's going to be edited, and what it's going to look like. And I could be doing a scene where I think it's scene ninety-four, it might end up being scene two-hundred and thirteen. So with the best will in the world, you have to commit, but also be open. That's the hard thing. Because if you think, "I'm going to do this scene, this scene means this, it's all these characters, and it's this moment..." it might not even be there, clearly, 'cause that's the nature of film-making, or it might be somewhere else. And he's pretty open about that.'

Freeman liked how Jackson tells stories; his style of film-making. The New Zealand director was easy to work with – he doesn't have the workhorse reputation that precedes someone such as James Cameron. Freeman does not believe in making life any more difficult than it needs to be. Everyone involved in the film had a job to do and they were all there to help tell the story, Jackson most of all. A film is in many ways a negotiation between the director and the cast – if the director does not get what he wants, until he sees on screen what is the right thing, it's down to the cast to help realise that vision. Actors don't want to walk off-set questioning if they've done the right thing or not. They may have done what's on the script but is it exactly what the director envisaged? Actors have to please everyone – the crew, the studio heads, the audiences, the critics. Actors are contractually obligated to please the director but they have an artistic plan to please themselves.

The Hobbit: An Unexpected Journey was finally completed on 26 November 2012, just two days before its Wellington premiere. The anticipation was high.

This film was Freeman's second major literary film adaptation, with the first, of course, being *The Hitchhiker's Guide to the Galaxy*. So how did the experience of filming these two projects compare with each other? There was a great deal more green screen time ('green screen acting' means acting alone in front of a green screen, with camera devices that make certain characters look different sizes – some consider it disorientating) working with Peter Jackson on *The Hobbit* but the stories are set in completely different universes and both experiences were unlikely to ever be repeated.

Martin spoke to journalists at the 2012 Comic-Con about his experiences on set: '…just for breadth of scale and time, and being in a different part of the hemisphere than I'm used to. It's a whole different experience. It's like a huge chunk of your life. That, alone, makes it different from anything else. The budget makes it different. You're constantly walking onto sets and sound stages where what you're acting on would take up the entire budget of any other film I've done. So, just the scale of it is quite phenomenal. For me, they're incomparable.'

Freeman probably wanted nothing to do with green screen acting before *The Hobbit* but he understands that many big-budget Hollywood films use green screens and that whatever is in the background near the acting will be inserted using computer-generated imagery.

'The reality is though that the most traditional part of acting is using your imagination,' he explained to UK's *Ask*

Men's Jamie Watt. 'It's what I was doing when I was five and it's what I'm doing now that I'm, er, twenty-eight… Using your imagination is the key to any kind of performance, so when it came to the green screen, I was surprised. I thought it would drive me mad, but the sets were usually a mix of the virtual and the physical – stuff we could touch, taste and smell, so it didn't seem like the whole time we were speaking to tennis balls. There was some of that, but there was also some actual material. If you look around Bag End, in Bilbo's house, it's all real, it's all tangible, so it's nice to have that mixture.'

On the experience of working with green screen, Freeman said to 3 *News*'s Kate Rodger, 'Acting is pretending so you just have to pretend. It's not as much fun as when someone else is there. When someone else is there, that's really fun, and that's when I think truly great things can happen. When you're doing it on your own it is less fun, because it's less organic and you're having to manufacture more. But it's just a matter of digging deep into your imagination. It's your idea of how the dragon is going to be massive, terrifying and it's going to have this booming voice coming out that will scare the bejeezus out of him.'

Arthur Dent and Bilbo Baggins are both reluctant heroes who are thrown into a dangerous adventure. There's a nervous energy about them as well as a bland ordinariness yet an underlying strength, which made perfect casting for Freeman.

'With Arthur Dent, he serves, I suppose, a similar function to Bilbo, in that he's the nearest thing to an audience member, in the film,' Freeman explained to reporters at Comic-Con in 2012. 'He's the audience's way in. And to a certain extent, you could argue that they're archetypes, in the hands of a much lesser actor. Cue laughter. They're ciphers, in a way, I suppose you could say.'

The role would change some significant parts of his life: his bank balance and fame being two primary factors. He'd been famous in London for a decade, where people would chat to him in the street, question him about *The Office*, ask for photographs and autographs but he'd never had that in Spain or France. So being internationally famous was an entirely different ball game. Freeman had been cast in many independent films with little distribution but *The Hobbit* was going to be shown all around the world and, as such, his privacy would be compromised. He knew that when he took on the role.

There was an enormous marketing campaign. The very first trailer was released before *The Adventures of Tin Tin*, produced by Jackson, in the US on 21 December 2011. Jackson, along with Freeman, McKellen and others, appeared at the San Diego Comic-Con International in 2012 to promote the film and a screening of twelve minutes' footage. Such was the level of euphoria in New Zealand that on 8 October 2012 Wellington Mayor Celia Wade-Brown announced that the New Zealand capital would be renamed 'Middle of Middle Earth' for the week of the film's premiere.

'It's kind of weird when everywhere you go there are pictures of you,' said Freeman to the *Daily Telegraph*'s John Hiscock. 'It's certainly unusual for any film I've ever done. But it's a good picture of me and at least I'm happy with it, because if it was a picture I hated I wouldn't go out.'

The 2012 Comic-Con was his first experience of such an event. In terms of comic books and movies, the San Diego Comic-Con is the biggest social event on the calendar. Fans meet and greet some of their heroes, buy and sell merchandise, attend Q&As and watch previews of upcoming films. It's a major event with global publicity.

Freeman told reporters at the 2012 press conference, 'So in a way it's fulfilling my expectations of what I heard about Comic Con, and exceeding them as well. I was struck by just how emotional people were talking about the film, talking about anticipating the film. With each question came a preamble about what the previous films have meant in people's lives. So all clichés aside, it's a really nice thing to be part of something that actually touches people, genuinely touches people. It's quite a lovely thing.'

Martin joked that people had been annoying him in restaurants in the UK for years but with the imminent release of *The Hobbit* this attention will be with him all over the world. But that is the price actors pay for fame – for taking on such an iconic role in the first place.

'I'm getting a glimpse of that external reaction to it now, the nearer the film gets to release,' said the forty-one-year-old Freeman to the *New Zealand Herald*. 'I mean that level of fame obviously is something very different to what most people will get to experience, but my life doesn't feel any different yet.'

Released on 28 November 2012 in New Zealand and internationally on 13 December, *The Hobbit: An Unexpected Journey* grossed over $1 billion at the international box office, which surpassed both *The Lord of the Rings: The Fellowship of the Ring* and *The Lord of the Rings: The Two Towers*. It was the fourth-highest grossing film of the year and the seventeenth-highest grossing film of all time. Martin Freeman was now box-office gold.

The movie was such a success that Freeman was worried it would change his life more than he anticipated.

'I remember having those conversations before *The Hitchhiker's Guide to the Galaxy* came out [in 2005] and thinking, fuck, is everything going to change?' he said to *Time Out London*'s Nick Aveling. 'And it didn't, really. I'm a big believer that life changes as much as you want it to. If you invite in all the madness, it will. If you don't, if you kind of let the world quietly know, "No thanks, I still want to get on the train and live my own life," then somehow it doesn't have to.'

Empire magazine's Dan Jolin enthused, 'His Bilbo does take his predicament seriously, and while this is the jauntiest – at times silliest, at times funniest, certainly the most child-friendly – Middle-earth movie yet, Freeman remains its emotional lodestone.'

He continued, 'Jackson holds on Freeman's face. This isn't just Tim-from-*The Office* or Watson in pointy ears, but an actor at the height of his prowess finding every layer to a character it now seems he was born to play.'

Total Film magazine's Matthew Leyland wrote: 'Elijah Wood's Frodo may have carried an incalculable burden but he was, frankly, a bit of a whinger. Freeman's Bilbo likes a moan too, but the part gives the Brit licence to show off his sitcom-honed comic touch.'

He continued, 'He also straddles the tone's comic/dramatic

divide. Just when you worry his self-effacing performance is getting lost in the monster mash, along comes the centrepiece confrontation with Gollum (Andy Serkis, showstopping as ever), a game of riddles where Bilbo's wit and mettle are shaded with genuine anxiety.'

Philip French of *The Observer* wrote, 'Bilbo (Ian Holm, reprising his role from *The Lord of the Rings*) is seemingly writing his memoirs, puffing on his churchwarden pipe and blowing out smoke rings as big as haloes and eating regular meals. As he contemplates the past he's replaced by his equally pacifist younger self, to which part Martin Freeman brings the same decent, commonsensical, very English qualities that informed his excellent Dr Watson on TV.'

The role of Bilbo Baggins won Freeman acclaim as well as some awards and nominations. He picked up Best Hero at the 2013 MTV Movie Awards and Best Actor at the eighteenth *Empire* Awards as well as Visionary Actor at the Short Awards. Freeman was also nominated for Hottest Actor at the 2012 *Total Film* Hotlist Awards and Best Actor at the following year's Saturn Awards as well as Best Scared-as-Shit Performance at the MTV Movie Awards, Best Actor at the *SFX* Awards, Hero Of The Year at the New Zealand Movie Awards, Best Male Performance In A 2012 Science Fiction Film, TV Movie, Or Mini-Series at the Constellation Awards, Best Leading Actor at the Tumblr Movie Awards and Best Ship at the Tumblr Movie Awards.

'I'm geek royalty now,' he joked with *Hollywood Reporter*'s Jordan Zakarin. 'That's the main responsibility. It's not playing Bilbo, it's my responsibility as a geek prince.'

Jon Plowman, the former head of comedy at the BBC and

executive producer of *The Office* knows how well Freeman can act when he's cast in the right roles. 'He's great at playing the everyman, which is why he is so good as Watson and in *The Hobbit*. He's got a wonderful ordinariness which you'd think most actors would have but curiously they don't. That's not an insult – it's the absolute opposite – and if you've got it as an actor you bloody well hang on to it.'

Such was the hype surrounding the film that its success was surely going to upset Freeman's relatively peaceful life. How could he possibly stay relaxed with the inevitability of worldwide fame?

'Until it actually happens it's all an intellectual exercise,' he said to John Hiscock of the *Daily Telegraph*. 'What if everyone hates it? I try not to count my chickens but yes, it's clearly a bigger film than I've ever made. People are so enthusiastic about this story that if I thought about them hating it or hating my rendition of it I wouldn't be able to go to work.'

The Hobbit is one of the productions Freeman is proudest of and it's probably going to be the one film he will speak fondly of in decades to come.

Freeman had Arthur Dent, John Watson and Bilbo Baggins to his name: three iconic characters of literature. How did he feel?

'I'm very proud of all of that,' he expressed to *Digital Spy*'s Morgan Jeffery. 'It is a weird thing at the moment to be Bilbo Baggins and John Watson. I can't deny that it's quite strange. I never think about it, but when it's put like that, I think "Christ, that is odd." They are iconic roles, but it's all accidental and it's all happenstance. I certainly don't think there's a casting director somewhere going, "How do we get Martin the iconic roles?"'

There was never any plan to immerse himself in any of these projects. He didn't wake up one morning and wonder what adaptation he would tackle next. It all happened by accident and, as the writing was so good, he could not turn any of them down.

Freeman was not daunted by taking on these iconic roles – not through arrogance or some self-absorbed higher belief in his own talent but rather because being scared would be counter-productive. Also, he was not steeped in the work of Conan Doyle, or Tolkien or Douglas Adams.

'I think it's this simple thing about, I came to this job, this profession, out of joy and out of play, and I know no one's going to die, however shit I am, do you know what I mean? It's okay,' he admitted to *Collider*'s Steve 'Frosty' Weintraub. 'I'd rather not be shit, obviously, I'd rather be good. Genuinely, it's crushing if people don't like me, but as with everything, I'm the ultimate judge of my work. I can only say, "Well, I liked it," or, "I didn't like it," and there are some times when I didn't like it. But no, I'm honestly not, I'm really not. I'm daunted by so many other things in life, work is not one of them. I'm daunted about almost everything else, it's a constant cause of fucking concern to me. But work is just not one of them at all, yeah. I don't worry about work. And that's partly 'cause I've been lucky and I've always worked.'

'So many British people with no prospects say, "I'm going to go to Hollywood and just see what happens,"' he said to *Movie Web*'s Julian Roman. 'And I'm like, "What the fuck do you think

THE UNEXPECTED ADVENTURES OF MARTIN FREEMAN

is going to happen?" That's the place where everyone wants to be. And if you're making *The Godfather* that's great. But you can make rubbish at home! Good scripts wherever they come from is what I'm interested in.'

Hilariously, a spoof video of *The Office* creator and lead actor Ricky Gervais as Gandalf The Grey went viral. *The Office: An Unexpected Journey* takes footage from *The Hobbit* film and superimposes the voices and faces of characters from *The Office*. Obviously it is a nod to Freeman's casting in both creations. The video starts with Gervais as *The Office* manager David Brent dressed as Gandalf delivering one of his more famous lines from the show: 'People say I'm the best boss, they go, "Oh, you get the best out of us," and I go, "C'est la vie." Freeman is obviously Bilbo Baggins and offers some lines from *The Office*, and there's a small role from Ewen MacIntosh (Big Keith in *The Office*) and, even funnier, Mackenzie Crook (Gareth Keenan in *The Office*) is Gollum. The video was mashed up by UK producers Jonny Lang and Jason Burke. They wrote on YouTube, 'Like *The Office*? Then you may well like this unique blend of those two worlds where David Brent (aka Gandalf The Grey) tells us all about his philosophy around running a regional parchment merchants in Middle-earth.'

The box-office success of *The Hobbit* has made Freeman a very wealthy man and that meant that he could dress sharply and afford bespoke suits from the revered tailor Mark Powell, who also designs suits for famed cyclist Bradley Wiggins. He's always had an eye for fashion but didn't always have the money to be able to afford nice clothes. Freeman is inspired by modernism both stylistically and musically. He likes modernism because it takes elements from everywhere and resists being a uniform. Another follower of this philosophy is Paul Weller, who dresses the same way he did decades ago.

Freeman loves the pre-mod jazz look of the 1950s to 1970s suedeheads (an offshoot of skinhead subculture). He is an avid fan of 1970s culture, whether it be the clothes, the music of The Jam, the comedy of The Goodies or the American films of Al Pacino. His other style influences would be Jerry Dammers of The Specials, Pete Tosh of The Wailers and, of course, Mr Paul Weller. Another hero of his is Steve McQueen. Martin has likened being a Mod with being a member of a cult in that people who are true Mods are vehemently dedicated to the cause. Being a Mod is about portraying yourself as an individual and not dressing in a uniform or whatever attire is currently in fashion. The cut of people's jeans, the tautness of the shirts, the hair, the shows – they all mean something to a Mod.

Paul Weller has had a profound impact on the Mod scene. As one of Britain's most respected and successful singer-songwriters, he started his career in The Jam, which he left in 1982 to branch out into the more soulful, less rock The Style Council from 1983 to 1989 before venturing into a solo career in 1991. He is often referred to as The Modfather and was a key figure in the revival of the Mod scene in the 1970s and 1980s. He is very much a British icon with his music rooted in British culture. Some of Freeman's musical influences overlap with Weller's, such as The Beatles, the Small Faces and various 1960s and 1970s soul artists like Stevie Wonder. Some of Weller's best known solo albums include *Stanley Road*, *Heavy Soul* and *Illumination*.

Weller and Freeman's mutual hero is the late Steve Marriott. He made a name for himself in two key British bands: Small Faces (1965–1969) and Humble Pie (1969–1975, 1980–1981). Marriott became a Mod icon during his tenure in the Small Faces. His influences were R&B, blues and soul singers from across the Atlantic, such as Ray Charles, Otis Redding, Muddy Waters, Buddy Holly and Booker T. & the M.G.'s. Marriott died in 1991 in an accidental fire at his sixteenth-century home in Essex, thought to have been caused by a cigarette.

With Fred Perry shirts, Levi jeans and a Small Faces mod-style haircut, Freeman is always seen impeccably dressed, though the same cannot be said of some of his on-screen characters, such as Tim Canterbury and Arthur Dent. Martin is especially a fan of loafers, which have been a fixture in his wardrobe since he saw Terry Hall of The Specials wearing them. He also likes coats, macintoshes, Crombies and Smedleys.

'You could say I'm a mod, but with a small "m"; I don't wear a parka, but I do question what I wear and what I listen to, which is what it's all about,' he admitted to the *Daily Mail*'s Chris Sullivan.

He added, 'Most actors are either a shower of bloody scruffs or think they should dress like Hamlet offstage. There's a lot of billowy shirtsleeves going on. But there aren't many Mods. Being a Mod is more of a sensibility than a style. It's hard explaining something that on the surface is rather silly and inexplicable.'

Mod-style has become fashionable again as far as the mainstream is concerned because of fans such as Freeman and cyclist Bradley Wiggins.

'I've been into what I've been into since I was about nine years old,' Freeman told *ShortList.com*. 'I started buying 2 Tone records, and from there went that rude boy sort of skin/mod/ soul boy route all my life. And I've always loved clothes. Even before I had money, I went charity shopping. So I've always had an eye for clothes.'

Sadly, Martin doesn't think the Mod subculture travels especially well across the Atlantic, as he told the *Metro*'s Andrew Williams: 'In Britain, even if people don't dress like that, everyone knows what they mean by a Mod and all these other subcultures, but they just don't know that in America. Given it's an acquired taste here, at least people know what people mean by it. When I am in America I feel, clothes-wise, like a fish out of water. It's a human need to fit in and you don't want people looking at you like you're a mental case. You feel like popping into Abercrombie & Fitch to buy a T-shirt to fit in. If you're wearing a flowery shirt over there people think you must either be mental or wanting to be beaten up for being gay. Fortunately, in London that's not the case. Too many people here wear fucking sports gear but everyone in America wears that, it's fucking everywhere. You don't see many pairs of trousers or shoes in America. It doesn't have much to offer me.'

Freeman loves the attention to detail that goes into making a tailored suit.

'The long march that we've all done towards tracksuit

bottoms and hoodies and trainers the entire time?' Freeman told *GQ*'s Oliver Franklin. 'I'm not having it. I like people making an effort for themselves and those around them.'

As well as tailor Mark Powell, Martin likes the label Albam, which opened its first shop in Soho in 2006. Freeman's best piece of advice when it comes to clothing is that anything will suit you so long as it fits. If the sleeve is an inch too long or the waist is an inch too short, the whole piece will fail and it won't look good. Freeman is rather militant when it comes to precision. He doesn't have a stylist because he knows about clothes and loves them. He thinks that, if a celebrity wins a Best Dressed award but doesn't know about clothes, it's because they have a stylist who does know about clothes and so it should be them that wins the award.

Asked about his shopping habits, he confessed to the *London Evening Standard*'s Hannah Nathanson, 'Albam on Beak Street, a men's outfitters I use for contemporary clothes with a traditional twist. For suits I go to the tailor Mark Powell who's been in Soho for about twenty-five years. I'll wear John Smedley till I die so I love the flagship store on Brook Street. I sometimes pop into Richard James on Savile Row. I devote far too much time and energy to clothes.'

As with his taste in music, Freeman tries to keep an open mind about fashion but there are some crimes against fashion that he simply cannot forgive.

'I've gone on dates with people when I was younger and you see them come over the escalator and you think, "No, this is not going to happen." You know: cowboy boots. No way, no fucking way,' he told *Esquire*'s Michael Holden in 2012.

Despite Freeman's growing fame, he remains grounded, incredibly polite (despite a professed love of swearing) and totally comfortable and at ease with himself. He is not an average Joe though – far from it. He is exceedingly witty and considerate with his responses and is aware of his talent. He is not an actor with a gigantic ego. He remains steadfastly British and approachable. His commitment to his profession has led him to some of the most memorable roles in popular culture over the past decade and it is certainly a testament to his talent that he has never been out of work. The scripts keep coming in, the phone is always ringing and there's no question that he is one of Britain's greatest actors of the early twenty-first century. Just what will he do next?

CHAPTER EIGHT

BACK TO MIDDLE EARTH

'I like the odd day on my own in the course of a
film because you've got complete control and you can
indulge yourself and all that sort of stuff.'
FREEMAN SPEAKING TO ANDREW ANTHONY
IN *THE OBSERVER*, 2014

Since *The Office*, Freeman appeared on several panel shows, such as as *Shooting Stars* and *Never Mind the Buzzcocks*, as well as popular talk shows like *Friday Night with Jonathan Ross*, *Parkinson*, *The New Paul O'Grady Show*, *This Morning*, *The Justin Lee Collins Show*, *The Five O'Clock Show* and *The Graham Norton Show*. He also appeared twice on the *Late Show with David Letterman*, one of the most popular late-night talk shows in America. Though he tried to shun the spotlight, there was no way around it.

Consequently, Freeman may be worth a staggering $10 million and have a shrewd business eye for finances but his long-term life partner is not quite as financially secure.

In March 2013 Abbie Abbington was declared bankrupt by London's High Court after failing to pay a huge tax bill but she refused to let her millionaire partner pay off her debts.

She confessed to the *Radio Times* in May, 'It was just me not managing my finances properly. I was putting some money away [to pay tax], but not all of it. I was working one year and not working another year. So I was using the money I'd saved… It will be annulled in a couple of months.'

She said that she is an only child (born in north London to Patsy and John Abbington) and is more than capable of looking after herself and does not want to rely on her partner and be seen in the eyes of the public as 'Freeman's girlfriend'.

'I know she copped it and it hurt,' Freeman explained to *The Independent*'s Emma Jones in 2013. 'It's been said before so it's a cliché, but it happens to be true: you can stand anything for yourself, but when they turn on the people you love, it's excruciating and it's invasive, no question about it. I do think we have a right to privacy. My job as an actor is for you, so why should my private life be for you too? That's not fair. Fortunately, apart from this, I am not that fascinating for the tabloids. I don't need their approval. There are about twenty people in my life that I want to love me, and none of them are the *Daily Mail*.'

There were speculations in the press that the pair had already married. It's never been publicly confirmed but they have alluded to it in interviews. Freeman spoke to the *London Evening Standard*'s Hannah Nathanson in 2010 for a piece on social life called 'My London'. When asked where he has had his favourite meal in the capital, he responded, 'My wife Amanda and I celebrated our wedding anniversary at Claridge's. It's quiet, not very showbiz and people do things properly there. I like being called Mr Freeman occasionally.' (Note that he refers to Abbington as his wife, though they have never publicly announced their marriage. It remains a cause of interest among the tabloid journalists as to whether or not they are actually married.)

Another piece of news was that she'd had a benign lump removed from her breast while Freeman was filming *The Hobbit* in New Zealand. Martin was desperate to travel the 11,000 miles back home to be with Abbington while she underwent surgery but she insisted he stay in New Zealand.

She told Rob Bleaney of the *Daily Mirror*, 'I said I'd be fine, but he was desperately worried. It was horrible for him. I found the lump after dropping the kids at school. I was sent to a specialist breast unit. They said they needed to get it out quickly because they didn't know if it was malignant. I burst into tears and thought, "Oh no. I'm going to die. I won't see my children grow up."'

There was an agonising two-week wait for the biopsy results, during which time Freeman sent her a bracelet and ring with a little note saying he hoped it would cheer her up. She thought it was a beautiful sentiment. When the results came back, she burst into tears as it was discovered to be a benign milk-gland tumour. She flew out to New Zealand with their two kids to be with Freeman. During their stay in that country Sir Ian McKellen babysat for them and read *The Gruffalo* to their two children, Joe and Grace.

Martin played Dr Williams in the short film *The Voorman Problem* produced by Honlodge Productions in the UK and directed by Mark Gill, who co-wrote the screenplay with Baldwin Li. It is based on a section of the acclaimed novel *number9dream* by David Mitchell.

There was a long six-week pre-production where the creative time found it a challenge to accommodate the cast's hectic schedule. Director Mark Gill spoke to *IndieWire*'s Carlos Aguilar: 'We were very confident on our script, so we decided to approach some great actors, the first one we approached was Kevin Spacey. We just wrote him a nice letter and he responded very positively saying that he would like to help, he suggested we contacted Tom Hollander directly and not use his agent, which is something you are not supposed to do but it worked for us. Then Tom and I had a conversation and Martin's name came up and we thought he'd be great. Tom sent Martin's agent an email with the script, and Martin's agent said yes. Sounds quite simple, but it really was that easy.'

In the film Freeman's character takes on the role of a prison psychiatrist after 'The War In The East' has produced a shortage of doctors. Williams is hired by Governor Bently. However, there is a prisoner named Voorman (played by Tom Hollander) who is adamant that he is God and has convinced the rest of the prisoners to spend all day chanting in worship. Due to a computer error, it is not known why Voorman is behind bars. This man, in a straitjacket, is interviewed by Williams in a locked room within the confines of the prison. Voorman explains that he is God and created the world exactly nine days ago. Naturally, Williams thinks this is the thought process of a loony and objects to the idea so Voorman suggests that, to test his powers, he will eliminate Belgium. Williams sits at home and tells his wife about the case. However, his wife has no idea what Belgium is so he gets out an atlas and points to where Belgium should be. It is a body of water called 'Walloon

Lagoon'. Williams is totally bewildered by this but does not believe Voorman. The latter suggests that he be the psychiatrist and Williams be God. They change attire – Voorman wears a suit and Williams puts on a straitjacket. Williams shouts out to the guards and, as Voorman leaves, he tells Williams to 'keep an eye on North Korea'. Voorman exits the room as the prisoners are heard chanting, a sound which gets louder as the film ends.

An intriguing little film, it was nominated for the Academy Award for Best Live Action Short Film in 2014 and was nominated for a BAFTA Award. It had a limited release on 23 April 2013 after being shown in Canada in August of the previous year.

Freeman wrapped up his appearances in the *Three Flavours Cornetto Trilogy* by appearing in the final film in 2013, *The World's End*. Freeman had a non-speaking role as Yvonne's boyfriend, Declan, in *Shaun of the Dead* and a cameo as a police officer in *Hot Fuzz* and now the trilogy was complete as he starred as Oliver Chamberlain, one of Gary King's (played by Pegg) friends in the final film.

Speaking about Freeman's character in the film, Edgar Wright told Simon Brew of *Den of Geek*, 'In the case of [Martin Freeman's] Oliver character, there's more than one kid at school who was destined to be a great businessman. And I think I was ever so slightly jealous of they because they seemed to have it all figured out, even at the age of sixteen. They know what they're doing, they understand finance and business. They've gone on to be very successful. So there's an element of me feeling like a little kid next to these guys. In fact one of them, just like the movie, was the first person I ever saw with a mobile phone. This was in 1991, and I was like what is that thing that kid has got?'

A science-fiction comedy directed by Edgar Wright and written by him – he had written the original draft when he was twenty-one and named it *Crawl* – and Simon Pegg, *The World's End* is the weakest of the films. It stars Pegg and Nick Frost as well as Paddy Considine, Pierce Brosnan and Eddie Marsan. The film's premise is simple: a group of mates discover an alien invasion during a pub crawl in their home town. Wright's influences included John Wyndham books in general and *Invasion of the Body Snatchers*. Freeman personally has no interest in pub crawls or a live-now, die-young lifestyle, preferring to stay at home with his partner or have a meal and do a pub quiz with friends.

Filming mostly took place at Elstree Studios Letchworth Garden City and Welwyn Garden City in Hertfordshire with some shots taken in High Wycombe railway station in Buckinghamshire, after principal photography commenced on 28 September 2012.

Freeman had been friends with Pegg and Frost for years and they each watched their respective careers flourish in different ways. Pegg enticed Martin to star in the film because of where it was shot – Freeman did not have to travel too far from his Hertfordshire home.

'It was part of the sugar pill to do the movie – "please sign up and we promise you'll never have to travel more than half an hour to work." That and the fact Simon and Edgar begged me to do it,' he said to *The Independent*'s Emma Jones in 2013.

The rule was that anyone who was in both *Shaun of the Dead* and *Hot Fuzz* had to return for *The World's End* regardless of how small their part might be.

'… with Martin Freeman,' Edgar Wright told *Dork Shelf*'s Andrew Parker, 'after *Shaun* and *Hot Fuzz*, we knew we HAD to get him back and give him a bigger part. It's great having these people back and giving them something to do because they're all really talented comedians.'

The World's End received its premiere on 10 July 2012 in London's Leicester Square and was released nationally on 19 July and in the US on 23 August. Its UK box-office takings were strong: it earned £2,122,288 during its opening weekend, which was higher than *Shaun of the Dead* but lower than *Hot Fuzz*, and it lost the top spot to *Monsters University*. It grossed $3.5 million on its opening day in the US and eventually made more money than the previous *Cornetto* films. The film won Best Ensemble Cast Award at the Alternative End Of Year Film Awards.

Reviews of the film were mostly positive, though some critics took swipes at it. There is a general consensus among fans of the films that it is the weakest link in the trilogy with less gags that hit the mark. Still, though Freeman's role was only minor, it was another string to his bow.

London Evening Standard's David Sexton wrote, 'So this one's easy to decide about: if you loved *Shaun* and *Hot Fuzz*, don't hesitate. You need some affection for men who are having problems growing up, perhaps. And maybe it is just very British to prefer the spoof to the original? Perhaps it was a mistake to watch it stony sober at a morning screening. It is still pleasing to think of all the less enlightened nations around the world being so fully informed at last of just what a proper pub crawl looks like.'

Though on the surface Freeman may not have anything in common with Pegg and his co-conspirators Nick Frost and Edgar Wright – self-appointed pop-culture geeks and comic-book nerds – it was certainly a wise move to be a part of the *Three Flavours Cornetto Trilogy*. Add that to *The Hobbit* and Martin Freeman, whether he appreciates it or not, is now firmly a member of the 'Geek Universe' for want of a better term.

Pegg is not only a colleague but a friend. His own career has taken off in unlikely directions and it's good to see both Freeman and Pegg enjoying their own turn in the spotlight. Pegg, born in Gloucestershire in 1970, carved an interesting career for himself post-*Spaced* and *Shaun of the Dead*. He struck up an unlikely friendship with director J.J. Abrams and was cast not only in *Star Trek* and *Star Trek Into Darkness* as Montgomery Scott (aka Scotty) but also as Benji Dunn in the third and fourth *Mission: Impossible* films. He was also cast in the Peter Jackson and Steven Spielberg film *The Adventures of Tintin* and, perhaps more surprisingly, he cropped up on the small screen in the Frank Darabont 1940s LA-noir series *Mob City*, which was unfortunately cancelled after one series.

Their mutual mate and colleague Nick Frost, meanwhile, may not have enjoyed as high-profile a career as Freeman or Pegg but he has starred in some projects of worth. He played drug dealer Ron in the awesome British sci-fi alien-invasion thriller *Attack the Block* and also starred in various roles in the sketch show *Man Stroke Woman*. His role as Jeremy Sloane in the series *Mr Sloane* won him critical praise, as did his performance as John Self in the adaptation of Martin Amis's acclaimed novel *Money* in the BBC TV movie of the same name in 2010.

Director Edgar Wright co-wrote, produced and directed the 2010 movie *Scott Pilgrim vs. the World* based on the cult comic books. He also co-wrote (with Joe Cornish and Steven Moffat) *The Adventures of Tintin*. For some time he was involved with the much-anticipated and written about Marvel superhero film *Ant-Man* but left the project.

There's no question that despite being on screen for only a short time, Freeman had pivotal roles in the three films and it proves again just how eclectic his body of work is.

There wasn't just a euphoria around the release of *The World's End* in July; it was announced by Peter Jackson on his Facebook page that the final scene featuring Bilbo Baggins had been filmed. It was probably a bittersweet moment: they were no doubt pleased that the long and arduous journey had come to an end and Freeman was probably ecstatic that he could fly back home to be with his family but at the same time the visiting cast and crew had a wonderful time in New Zealand, which they would miss. Fans were now looking forward to the release of *The Hobbit: The Desolation of Smaug* on 13 December 2013.

On 12 July 2013 Peter Jackson wrote, 'Tonight Martin Freeman finished his last shot as Bilbo Baggins… The end of an incredible two-and-a-half years. I cannot imagine anyone else in this role – a character that Martin has nurtured and crafted with love and great skill.

'We have said goodbye to our elves, humans, wizards and now the hobbit. We now enter our final 2 weeks of pick-ups, and it's wall-to-wall dwarves.

'These pick-ups have been gruelling and intense, but I'm so happy with what we've been shooting. These next two movies are going to be pretty great!'

While Freeman will miss the cast and crew of *The Hobbit*, he won't miss the rigmarole of putting on Bilbo's costume. He had to shave his legs, and talcum-powder them for the flipper-like Hobbit feet. He put an inner-sole in the shoe then put a latex leg and foot over it to make him look like a hobbit. It was a two-person job that took around a fortnight to get used to. Shooting three movies back-to-back in another country while flying back home to work on *Sherlock* was hard work. It was eighteen months that required Freeman to be fit and healthy. Back in London there was a period of decompression; a feeling of returning to normality.

2013 was a productive year, not only with the release of *The World's End* but also *Svengali*, in which he played Don, and he voiced the character of Bernard D. Elf in *Saving Santa*.

Svengali is a British film about a postman from South Wales named Dixie (played by Jonny Owen) who is a music fanatic and dreams of discovering a great band to rival the best. One day while trawling through YouTube videos he stumbles across The Premature Congratulations. He tracks them down and offers to be their manager. He gets them to record a demo so he can shop it around the London record labels. The story follows Dixie's journey around the London music industry. His partner is Michelle (played by Vicky McClure), who helps him on his quest and he struggles to deal with egos and the general issues of band management. As the band's success grows, his chances of continuing to manage them decrease. He is divided in his loyalties: a life as a band manager – something he has always dreamed of – or a life with Michelle. Directed by John Hardwick, *Svengali* had been screened at the sixty-seventh Edinburgh International Film Festival on 21 June 2013 and nominated for the Michael Powell Award, which honours best British feature films. It later had a UK release on 21 March 2014. The film has since all but disappeared from recent memory.

In a one out of five-star review in *The Guardian*, Jonathan Romney wrote, 'With sparky prestige support (Martin Freeman, Maxine Peake, Matt Berry) and cameos from Alan McGee and Carl Barât, *Svengali* ought to be sharper, but this good-natured, clunky labour of love feels about as fresh as a 2002 copy of the *NME*.'

Total Film's Kevin Harley wrote, 'Likeable casting can't quite salvage director John Hardwick's threadbare British pop comedy, under-developed from a web series… Martin Freeman's grumpy shop-owner and several pop cameos (label maverick Alan McGee, The Libertines' Carl Barat) play like sketch matter, better suited to this spread-thin project's online origins.'

Freeman was presented with a fellowship by the members of University College Dublin's Literary & Historical Society on 5 October 2013. The campus's Fitzgerald Chamber was filled to capacity as students sat to listen to Martin give an engrossing talk about his successful career. He even posed for photos with guests and his framed accolade.

Saving Santa is a computer-animated comedy created and

written by Tony Nottage and directed by Leon Joosen. It's about an elf who is the only one of Santa's elves that can stop the invasion of the North Pole by using the secret of Santa's sleigh, a TimeGlobe, to track back in time – twice – to save Santa. The film also stars Tim Curry, Joan Collins and Chris Barrie. It was released in the US on 5 November 2013 and went to DVD in the UK and has since faded into the mists of time.

Total Film's Neil Smith wrote, '"Once something is done, it cannot be undone!" declares Father Christmas in *Saving Santa*, an amateurish cartoon that'll have you fervently hoping the opposite.'

The Observer's Mark Kermode wrote, 'That Martin Freeman and Tim Curry (both mighty in their own way) should lend their voices to this let-down is depressing enough; that Joan Collins and Ashley Tisdale have been roped in somehow makes it worse. On this evidence, Santa's sadly not worth saving.'

It had been a year since the release of the first *Hobbit* film, so was Freeman prepared to enter the world of cult fandom and become an icon to millions?

'There hasn't actually been as much craziness as you would think, or at least as much as I was prepared for,' he admitted to 3 News's Kate Rodger. 'There's actually more *Sherlock* craziness in my life. Weirdly, I think it manifests itself more from *Sherlock* than it does from *Hobbit* people. *Hobbit* people have been very restrained, actually and the ones who are really on it are *Sherlock* folks. But yeah, people occasionally say 'Bilbo' when they see me. There's a very broad appeal, age-wise, to *The Hobbit*. If a nineteen-year-old girl is coming up to me, that'll be *Sherlock*. If it's an eight-year-old boy, it'll be *The Hobbit*.'

The Hobbit: The Desolation of Smaug, the eagerly awaited sequel to *The Hobbit: An Unexpected Journey*, was premiered in LA on 2 December 2013 and released internationally on 11 December. The film follows the journey of Bilbo Baggins as he joins Thorin Oakenshield and his fellow dwarves on a quest to reclaim the Lonely Mountain from the dragon Smaug. Gandalf the Grey also investigates the evil forces at work at the ruins of Dol Guldur. The film features a stellar cast, joining Martin Freeman, including Ian McKellen, Richard Armitage, Benedict Cumberbatch, Evangeline Lilly, Lee Pace, Ken Stott, James Nesbitt, Orlando Bloom and Luke Evans.

Freeman spoke to *Flicks And Bits* about Cumberbatch's role in the film. The pair had both auditioned for their respective parts in London during the filming of *Sherlock* series one.

'He did the whole physical performance of it in a performance capture suit and all that,' Freeman explained, 'but given that he's not 200 ft tall and not the shape of a dragon, there's only so much you can do with that. But he brought such a fantastic vocal quality to it, which he has a fantastic range with – especially that lower registry. He's really good and very right for Smaug.'

Martin revealed that he never rehearsed with Cumberbatch for *The Hobbit: The Desolation of Smaug*. They were not even on the same continent.

'We knew what we were doing,' he said at a TV press interview. 'When we came back for the second or third series of *Sherlock*, he'd be saying, "I've got to go back and do more bits of Smaug." So, we knew what we were up to but never [in detail].'

'It was great,' Cumberbatch said to MTV News on working with Freeman on a different project other than *Sherlock*. 'I got to hang out with him, and I kept a straight face for a bit and then I started giggling because I know Martin, I don't know Bilbo. For Martin to be sitting there playing Bilbo is amazing. He's going to be amazing, he's going to be fantastic in this film.'

Bilbo is far more experienced by the second film and the process is gradual, which the audience are able to relate to. He's not an action hero or a heroic icon but he has seen many things he had not previously witnessed and he's come a long way since the journey began. He'd never even been in a fight but here he is on a major journey, coming across all manner of foes. He shows bravery and nobility that he probably wasn't even aware he had.

Speaking about his character in the second film, Freeman told *Flicks And Bits*, 'I really like Bilbo's innocence, and I like playing the change from innocence to experience. I like that. So that he has a figurative journey, as well as the literal one as he goes on. Every actor wants to play different things or beats within a moment, or beats within a scene. You don't want to be playing the same thing all of the time, and you certainly get that aspect of Bilbo, definitely in the second film. There's a person there with more iron in his backbone, I guess. He's just seen more, so his whole world view has shifted.'

Also, Bilbo is a flawed, slightly awkward and silly character. He's certainly not your typical hero.

'He is pompous and he is fairly small-minded,' Freeman explained to *AsiaOne*. 'So it's not like he can be James Bond. And from Bilbo's point of view, when he thinks he is being really serious, actually the world is going, "Prat!" because he is puffing himself up in a classically English pompous way. It is funny. Pete was always asking me to do "that English thing". I don't really know what that is.'

Martin Freeman was now, in the eyes of the public, Bilbo Baggins. The actor had fully immersed himself in the role and was very comfortable.

'Just the oddness of it, I think,' Freeman admitted to *Stuff. co.nz*'s Tom Cardy about the costume and prosthetics. 'But I suppose by the first time I'd seen myself in the monitor, I was used to it. I'd had so many fittings, and I'd had so many pictures taken, and so many versions of the costume, and versions of the wig. But yeah, it felt kind of odd. I look fairly different as Bilbo, but what's weird now, is it just doesn't feel strange at all. And I genuinely forget – we all forget what we look like.'

The Hobbit was originally slated to be a two-film project but a third feature was announced and so the second film was consequently renamed *The Hobbit: The Desolation of Smaug*. The screenplay was penned by Jackson with Fran Walsh, Philippa Bovens and Guillermo del Toro. It was shot in 3D with principal photography taking place in New Zealand and at England's legendary Pinewood Studios. Additional filming was scheduled for May 2013 and lasted for approximately ten weeks.

Freeman was juggling *Sherlock* series three and the second *Hobbit* movie. It was a hectic period for the actor.

'I always am around this time in the series,' Freeman said to Mark Gatiss in a special feature in the *Radio Times* dated January 2014. 'I think the schedules on this show are quite brutal – *The Hobbit* is a doddle, actually, comparatively. So yeah, I'm quite tired, but I have to say I'm enjoying it. I have to say I'm enjoying it. It's contractual!'

Freeman enjoyed the months spent filming in New Zealand but, of course, Wellington differs massively from the English capital. He certainly enjoyed the more laid-back, outside lifestyle of Wellington, though he loves London more than anywhere else in the world.

'Wellington is a pretty small place,' he told *AsiaOne*. 'It's easy. I mean, I love London more than anything else, but Wellington doesn't have the stress about it. It just doesn't. It would be impossible to be as stressed in Wellington as you are in London. If you are travelling fifteen minutes in Wellington then that's quite a long journey. I was travelling six minutes to work each day. Could you imagine that in London?'

How did he cope being so far from home?

'When you're working for very long hours through the days and nights it's easy not to look after yourself and not to eat and sleep properly,' he expressed to the *Daily Mirror*'s John Hiscock. 'So I had regular massages and without them I would have gone barmy.'

He continued, 'I love my home and part of the reason I love it is that it's private, so I don't want to talk about it. It's where I feel sane and where I feel safe, and I love it for that.'

Freeman especially enjoyed filming the fighting scenes with the Wargs, which are giant wolves kept by Orcs. Usually, however, those scenes involved the stunt team dressed in green-screen outfits carrying a head that Freeman had to stick a sword in, and the rest would be done with computer-generated imagery by the computer geeks.

'This is the film where Bilbo becomes totally invaluable to the group – he's not a mascot or someone to be patronised,' Freeman told *Time Out London*'s Nick Aveling on the progression of his character. 'In fact, he saves their arses on numerous occasions, so he's really needed. He finds more character, more backbone, than he knew he had. I love Bilbo's "plucky" side, but I'm also interested in when he has to get serious. In times of war, manners and politeness don't mean too much.'

Despite the abundance of special effects, stunts and action sequences, the writers were shrewd enough to include those tender human moments that audiences can relate to.

'… even though he [Peter Jackson] wants people to be able to escape into these worlds that he helps create, it is meaningless unless you cut back to what you really think or what you're really feeling about this,' Freeman expressed to James Rocchi of *MSN Entertainment*. 'So it's always the small bit I think. It's always the devil's in the details. And I think you need to kind of focus in on how is this person reacting to all this. That's why I love Pete's battles. The battles are never just about, "Yay, we're all goring each other to death." It's actually, you know, you cut back to a child and the fact that the child is terrified or the fact that Thorin has just seen his father's head cut off...'

The film had a major marketing campaign that dominated the entertainment media for much of the year. Jackson held a live event on 24 March 2013 in which he revealed some plot details and screened a scene from the film. The first trailer was released on 11 June 2013 and a longer trailer was shown on 4 November. A special live online fan event (hosted by CNN anchor Anderson Cooper in New York) was staged across eleven different cities on 4 November with Peter Jackson, Jed Brophy, Evangeline Lilly, Lee Pace, Orlando Bloom, Luke Evans, Andy Serkis and Richard Armitage. Freeman took part in the heavy marketing campaign by appearing on TV, radio and in various press events around the world.

Speaking to the *Radio Times*'s Susanna Lazarus about working with Freeman, Richard Armitage enthused, 'He was just very good at being a little ninja Bilbo. Behind the scenes he'd have a little crack at everybody who was a bit bigger than him but he'd try his kung fu ninja moves on everybody which always made me laugh.'

Not only was there a heavy promotional campaign but also a great deal of *Hobbit*-related merchandise, from action figures to posters and all manner of collectibles. *ShortList.com* spoke to Freeman about the *Hobbit*-branded bath and shower gel, to which the actor responded, 'Well, I haven't seen that... I occasionally get sent things, I occasionally get sent a new batch of... whatever... I think the majority of the stuff that happens in *The Hobbit* merchandise wise I honestly never see and I'm not really aware of that's the truth. I hear about stuff... I know the figures and I know books...'

The film premiered in Los Angeles on 2 December 2013 and was released around the world on 13 December. It grossed $953 million worldwide, surpassing the box-office takings of *The Lord of the Rings: The Fellowship of the Ring* and *The Lord of the Rings: The Two Towers*. It became the fourth-highest grossing film of 2013 and the twenty-fourth-highest grossing film ever. The reviews of the second *Hobbit* film were far more positive than those of *An Unexpected Journey*.

The Guardian's Peter Bradshaw wrote, 'Martin Freeman is Bilbo, and Freeman's laidback, more naturalistic line readings make a pleasing and interesting contrast to the more contoured saga-speak that comes out of everyone else's mouth, whether they are speaking English or Elvish or the guttural Orcish.'

Total Film's Matt Maytum wrote, 'Freeman does at least deliver the goods in some challenging early scenes that see Bilbo in thrall to the lure of the all-important One Ring, with a standout moment plumbing depths of moral murkiness rarely addressed in family entertainment.'

Empire's Nick de Semlyen wrote, 'As Bilbo (a still spot-on Martin Freeman) and co. near their destination, the film gets increasingly busy, splitting the group in two and intercutting between those strands and Gandalf (Ian McKellen), who's off poking around the ruins of Dol Guldur. That storyline still hasn't quite caught fire (it basically amounts to the wizard yelling at a giant, evil ink-blot), and it could be argued that more screen time might have been usefully given to the dwarves, who remain largely anonymous.'

Robbie Collin of the *Daily Telegraph* wrote, 'It even begins beautifully, with a too-rare bit of comic business from Freeman, whom you can't help feel more to offer the part of Bilbo than the film is prepared to give him room for.'

Freeman picked up a Stella Award for Best Actor In A Leading Role and was also nominated for Best Hero at the Comic Vine Movie Awards, MTV Movie Awards and YouReviewers Awards. At the time of writing, he was nominated for Best Male Performance In A 2013 Science Fiction Film, TV Movie, Or Mini-Series at the Constellation Awards.

It was revealed by the *Sunday People* that Prince William is a fan of *The Hobbit*. Speaking at the Olivier Awards for stage plays, the paper reported that Freeman said, 'He was a nice guy. He is the biggest royal fan. He knew all the facts about Middle Earth and obviously wanted to be there. Kate was in hospital at the time.'

During the promotional round of interviews, Freeman appeared on the UK's *The Graham Norton Show* with fellow guests Ben Stiller and Jamie Oliver. 'It's done, it's all finished – for however long you think you are going to be in a Peter Jackson film, you are going to be in it longer,' he told Norton.

'It was a long gig. My main challenge was checking in with Peter to see where Bilbo was at a given time. Two-and-a-half years is a very long time to keep a handle on it,' he continued.

Freeman was now a bona fide Hollywood star, not of A-list pedigree, mind you, but he was now a fully recognisable actor of the big and small screen, and also a national treasure.

'We all make films hoping people will come and see them and I've made plenty of films people didn't come and see, so it's nice to have things people do like,' he said, commenting on the worldwide success of *The Hobbit*.

CHAPTER NINE

FARGO AND THE RETURN TO BAKER STREET

'I do think – in a very real, common sense way – that if you
want to be famous, you can be. It's not a great talent; if you
put yourself forward, it will happen to you.'
FREEMAN SPEAKING TO NICK AVELING IN
TIME OUT LONDON, 2013

In January 2014 Steven Moffat announced that a fourth series of *Sherlock* had been commissioned and scripts were planned. Plot lines have already been developed for both series four and series five but it all depends on the schedules, not just of Freeman and Cumberbatch but also of writers Moffat and Gatiss. It's a hard show to get together because of the growing successes of the careers of each person involved, including the creators.

Series three was hugely successful and was met with great acclaim from fans and journalists. 'The Empty Hearse' was first shown on BBC1 on 1 January 2014 with 'The Sign Of Three' to follow on 5 January and 'His Last Vow' on 12 January. *Sherlock* is one of the most watched BBC dramas in a decade, if not the most watched, and certainly one of the most revered TV series of modern times.

Cumberbatch reportedly received a letter from the Sherlock Holmes Society about how they think he should play Holmes. People have ideas about how iconic roles should be played, especially characters such as Sherlock Holmes, but both Cumberbatch and Freeman had their own thoughts and were not going to be swayed by the opinions of the fans. They had absolute faith in writers Gatiss and Moffat.

As has often been the case with shows that have cult appeal and that are genre based, they attract people who are perceived as outsiders, even though there are millions of them. Genre fans are attracted to stories such as *Sherlock* and *The Hobbit* because they represent escapism from the modern world – it is total fantasy. Fans dress as Benedict Cumberbatch, such is the level of success of the show. Shows like *Sherlock* touch many people in different ways and Freeman and his co-stars find it very gratifying.

Curiously, three series of *Sherlock* only equal nine episodes, which is not very many, especially when you consider that US TV shows can run anything between half a dozen episodes per season to as many as twenty-four. It just goes to show the enormous cultural impact *Sherlock* has made on the global viewing public. As with all good TV series, *Sherlock* has become its own thing. It has taken on a life of its own. Of course, such success makes it harder for the writers to live up to the heightening expectations that build with each pending series.

As the success of the series has risen over the years, the logistics of filming on the streets in public has become increasingly difficult. When they film in North Gower Street in central London, where Holmes's flat is located, it's akin to filming in the theatre. As soon as the fans spot them, they start clapping and cheering. It gets distracting for all concerned. Fans – mostly female – stand behind the barriers and cheer at Cumberbatch and Freeman. During breaks in filming, they ask the two stars for autographs. Such is Freeman's appeal that he'd get just as many fans hounding him as Cumberbatch. Tabloids shot photos of fans behind barricades as they filmed the latest series. They even took photographs of the two lead actors sipping coffees and eating paninis during a break from filming.

Sherlock is a series that does not patronise its viewers. It tricks them, surprises them and makes them think.

'Actors bang on about this a lot, but it's true: sometimes there is proof that audiences aren't stupid, however much they're treated as such [laughs],' Freeman said to *ShortList. com*. 'Sometimes there are occasions where you go, "I get that, I totally get that." There are bits of *Sherlock* I have to catch up with. I have to work hard. "Hang on, what's this? How does this fucking work?"'

Two years had passed since Holmes faked his own death at the end of series two. It had fans gasping for more and the wait felt like an eternity. There was a period of mourning and then Watson tried to pick up the pieces and move on to create a fairly steady life until Holmes comes back into the picture and his world is shaken up again.

'His best friend has died horribly in front of him,' Freeman told the BBC of Watson, 'which took a long time to get over, but the way that his life has moved on is that he has fallen in love with Mary. He is leading a functional, normal-ish life really which doesn't have the highs and lows of his life with Holmes but is certainly a bit more steady. But there is a sadness with John which will always be with him when you lose someone that you love – he is slightly dulled by life.'

When Holmes comes back Watson is so overwhelmed, so taken aback by surprise and shock that he faints. As the story progresses the duo become sharper with each other; there is more bite to their reactions with one another. Watson also punches Holmes, which shows just how angry he was.

After the huge success of the first two series, Freeman was not complacent about the third one. The important thing for him was making sure that he did his job as best he could. There are many twists and turns in the series's narrative but Freeman was not always in possession of the full facts. He was given the plot devices more or less as the filming began so he saw everything as it happened. He was able to create his own theories on such things as Holmes's death. It also made things easier during interviews so that he wouldn't accidentally let slip important events.

'Other than that, apart from the fact that we've all got potentially big mouths and you can say too much and then feel like an idiot, you actually don't want to ruin people's surprises,' he told *Den of Geek*'s Louisa Mellor, 'because however much people say, "Oh go on, tell us," they wouldn't thank you for it once the show goes out, they'd think, "Oh, I didn't really want to know that." As a punter, I love not knowing stuff, I always get annoyed if I'm watching a film or something with somebody else who's going, "He's going to," or, you know. I'd rather feel stupid and find out than know an hour in advance.'

Freeman has seen his character go through some changes in the three series. He misses being in Afghanistan and being with his comrades, an aspect of his life which was explored in the first series. The closest thing he gets to a thrill is being Holmes's sidekick, but Watson has developed so much since the partnership first began.

'With this new series, he's also fallen in love,' he told Mark Gatiss in a *Radio Times* interview. 'He thought his best friend was dead. There's definitely a sort of light that goes out when you lose somebody you love, but now his life has moved on. He's in a real grown-up relationship, which he needed to be. So I think that we join John in a way a bit sadder because he lost a friend, a very good friend, but in a way more content, actually.'

Watson's love interest in the series, Mary Morstan, is none other than Freeman's real-life partner, Amanda Abbington. She is a hugely significant part of Watson's existence and becomes Mrs Watson.

The first time the conversation came up between Freeman and the writers about who would play Watson's wife was during series two.

'I said, "Well, to be honest, I think Amanda would be pretty good," and he goes, "That's exactly what we were thinking,"' Freeman said to *Vulture*'s Denise Martin. 'They knew she was able to be funny and engaging and just right. I mean, the last thing you want is to feel like you're being John and Yoko, but Amanda can do this all day long in her sleep. Of course, I love her, but I know also she's really fucking good. I wouldn't say she should play everything in the world, but as far as this casting, it's pretty good.'

Freeman and Abbington went to Mark Gatiss's house with Steven Moffat to watch *The Hound of the Baskervilles* and after the film finished Gatiss suggested they go in the kitchen to chat about the next series and the introduction of a new female character. To follow the trajectory of the original stories they needed a love interest for Watson.

She said to *The Independent*'s James Rampton in 2013, 'I thought they were going to ask me, "Do you have any ideas for this part? Which actress do you think works well with Martin? What about Penélope Cruz or Gwyneth Paltrow [two of Freeman's previous co-stars]?" In fact, what they said to me was, "We'd like you to play Mary." I probably got quite emotional at that point.'

Abbington even tried to talk them out of giving her the role but they were adamant that she should be cast in the series. Gatiss and Moffat thought it would be easy for the couple to act together. Her role is pivotal to Watson's therapy after Holmes's shocking comeback in 'The Empty Hearse'. She found Freeman easy to work with and, after all, he is her favourite actor and not just her partner. The two characters go on a journey together in the stories and Abbington felt blessed to be given the opportunity to be cast opposite Freeman. She told *The Independent*: 'He's so easy to work with and so creative. He brings something different to every single take. He is so on top of his lines that he can dig down and find a different angle every time. That really keeps you on your toes. Both characters go on a wonderful journey, and to do that with Martin was such fun.'

Freeman has described her as 'unpretentious, unfussy, clear

in her decision-making and not a drama queen' in an interview with the *Sunday Times*'s Benji Wilson.

What Abbington found challenging was being the third wheel between Freeman and Cumberbatch. She felt the pressure of the role because she had quite a few scenes with the two of them and found the famous scene where Holmes reveals himself to Watson after everyone assumed he was dead to be a real challenge.

'Ben and Martin have real chemistry,' she admitted to *The Independent*'s James Rampton, 'and I had to hold my own in the scenes with them. It was daunting – not necessarily to come between them, but to arrive as another dynamic.'

On working with her partner, Abbington enthused to *The Hollywood Reporter*'s Philiana Ng, 'I think he's one of our finest actors and I think he's just a joy to work with, as is Ben[edict Cumberbatch]. Their chemistry is fantastic, so coming into that was slightly daunting because they work each off each other so beautifully. I've worked with Martin on other projects. They were all very small parts, but this was the first part of any substance and depth.'

However, when it became public knowledge that Abbington would be cast alongside Freeman in the show, she received death threats on Twitter. As quoted in an article in the *Express* by Tom Morgan, Freeman responded by saying, 'To me, they're not fans of the show – they're fans of a show going off their heads.'

He continued, 'Obviously I love Amanda and I want everyone to react positively to her. She plays a fantastic character and brings a hell of a lot to the third series.'

What's interesting about Watson is seeing what he has learned from Holmes and he applies the knowledge and skills to solving clues himself with Holmes's approval.

'I think, as you saw snippets of when Sherlock and I are together, you saw very very small snippets of when Sherlock would occasionally say, "Well go on then, let's see what you've learned,"' Freeman told *Den of Geek*'s Louisa Mellor. 'I think John, by his own admission… probably compared to another normal person in a room might look quite impressive because of his time with Sherlock and just because of his forensic skill, but knowing how small his knowledge is compared to Sherlock's, I think he would feel quite insecure about that.'

Series three also saw a new villain with the Scandinavian actor Lars Mikkelsen who plays Charles Augustus Magnussen, Holmes and Watson's latest nemesis in the vein of Moriarty.

The series has made both lead stars household names and has proved that Britain is capable of making good telly at a time when there is so much interest in American series such as *Breaking Bad*, *The Wire*, *House of Cards* and *Game of Thrones*. It is a testament to the writers' talents that they created such an engrossing, engaging and well-written series as *Sherlock* even with a BBC budget. Ultimately, regardless of financial restraints, it's all down to the writing. Big-budget TV shows can be disastrous if the writing is bad (the Spielberg-produced *Terra Nova* being a case in point) but shows such as *Sherlock*, which have relatively small budgets by today's standards, turn out wonderfully because the writing is superlative.

San Francisco Chronicle's David Wiegand said, 'The performances are even better than in previous years, with brand-new but fully credible sides of Holmes's and Watson's characters. And the writing, by Moffat and Gatiss, is in a league by itself. Other shows may plateau or tread thematic water once they're successful, but so far, *Sherlock* has been, and remains, a great show that only gets even better.'

The Washington Post's Hank Stuever wrote, '*Sherlock* moves swiftly and intelligently but also a little too coldly, like a long commercial for better WiFi... Cumberbatch's take on Holmes's narcissism can come off as skeevishly robotic. If not for Freeman's deeper, more human work as Watson, the style would soon go sterile.'

Writing in *Variety*, Brian Lowery said, 'It all works thanks heavily to the chemistry between Cumberbatch and Freeman, which alternates between wide-eyed wonder and exasperation to the point of the good doctor calling his pal a "dickhead" and a "cock".'

One thing Freeman is aware of is the online community that is dedicated to depicting sexual and intimate scenes between Holmes and Watson. Ian McKellen, his *Hobbit* co-star, even sent him some pictures via email with a message 'Have you seen this dear?'

'I've always seen it as a point of principle not to be offended if people imply you're gay – so no, I've never given a shit,' Freeman admitted to *Time Out London*'s Nick Aveling on the subject. 'If I was offended, I'd kind of think, well what does that make me? I wouldn't want a fifteen-year-old kid thinking I'm ashamed of it. I'm not. If anything, it's kind of funny to see pictures of me and Ben doing whatever we're doing to each other – even if they're far from the truth. The only time I'm sort of bothered is when people get proprietary about it or think there should be a certain kind of reaction, like it needs to be in the National Gallery.'

Freeman continued to be very protective of his privacy. On a recent trip to Japan Benedict Cumberbatch had been greeted by cheering fans as though he was the reborn messiah, but that is not something Freeman has experienced. Of course, Martin is famous but he is not one of the industry's most recognisable figures. He does not go out of his way to stay anonymous but remains reluctant to give too much away in interviews.

'Whenever I've been anywhere else, I've not been chased by people – it depends where I am and how visible I am,' Freeman told *GQ*'s Oliver Franklin. 'You can still be reasonably invisible. Not that I want to be – despite what people may think I've not gone through life trying to be anonymous. At the same time I want to have my private life and you can't have that if people are screaming and shouting at you while you're in a restaurant. I don't mind standing out in some ways.'

LEGO The Hobbit: The Video Game was released on 8 April, which relives the adventures of the first two *Hobbit* films *LEGO* style. It features the voices of the original cast members.

'You know I just like it if it's good,' he explained to Steven Balbirnie of *The University Observer*. 'If it's something that someone's made up yesterday and the first thing is a screenplay and I love it then I'm in. If it's an adaptation of something that I like then I'm also in. It's always just about what that screenplay is like, because you could've had a terrible adaptation of any of those things, I mean you could've had a terrible adaptation of any of those beloved books and I wouldn't have wanted to do it.'

One script that had an instant 'yes factor' for Freeman was *Fargo*.

Martin appeared for the first time in a major American TV series as Lester Nygaard in the dark-comedy crime drama series *Fargo* in April 2014. Written by Noah Hawley and filmed in Calgary, *Fargo* is inspired by the much respected 1996 film of the same name by the Coen Brothers, who are also executive producers of the series. The premiere was seen on US TV by 4.5 million viewers.

Set in January 2006, the story concerns the mysterious loner Lorne Malvo (Billy Bob Thornton) who passes through Bemidji in Minnesota and meets oddball insurance salesman Lester Nygaard (Freeman) in a hospital waiting room. Malvo encourages Nygaard with violence and malice, which sets off a chain of unlikely murders. On the case is rookie Deputy Molly Solverson (Allison Tolman) and Duluth police officer Gus Grimly.

Freeman didn't even audition for the part – it was a straight offer. Hawley had seen something else Freeman had been in and was impressed that the actor was not all sweetness and light.

He admitted to the *Daily Telegraph*, 'I didn't audition for *Fargo*. It was a straight offer. They didn't even ask to hear the accent.' And then added, 'It could have all gone very, very bad. Yeah, I was surprised that they didn't want to hear that. 'Cause I could have had a cloth ear.'

Any reservations he had about the TV adaption of the

original movie went out of the window after reading the first script and the subsequent nine. Each script became more enthralling and surprising. Freeman found the characters, the setting, the overall story arc and subplots all very alluring. Fans of the original movie may have been dubious too, as it has a rather high cult status among movie buffs, but the film offered a different approach. They are two entirely different entities.

There is an anger in Freeman, something dwelling inside him that is waiting to burst into films. This anger is present in many of the great British actors, including Oliver Reed and Anthony Hopkins.

'Some of it is a sort of lighthearted anger that I know will pass,' admitted Freeman to Josh Rottenberg of *Entertainment Weekly*, 'but some of it is pretty deep-seated and a fundamental part of me that I think people often don't understand.'

His partner, his children and Martin's love of soul music and clothes give him periods of unmitigated glee but, 'it will probably never last that long without me puncturing it,' he continued to tell Rottenberg. 'It's a pain in the ass in some ways, and in other ways it's a blessing. For all of my faults as a person that it brings out, it's helped put food on the table.'

What impressed Freeman about the script was how impeccably written it was and how finely laced the story is with dark comedy, emotion and suspense. His decision to accept the role was based on the first episode, especially his character's first encounter with Billy Bob Thornton's mysterious loner, Lorne Malvo.

Speaking about Lester Nygaard, Freeman told Anne Bayley of *TwoCentsTV.com*, 'I just got the feeling that this was going to be a role where you could give rein to a lot of stuff, to play a lot of stuff. And even within that first episode the range that he goes between is really interesting and so I knew that was only going to grow and expand in the next nine episodes, and so it proved to be. In all the ten episodes I get to play as Lester pretty much the whole gamut of human existence and human feeling, you know, he does the whole lot. And that's exactly what you want to do as an actor.'

In terms of story development, Freeman knew very little about his character. There was much speculation about what Nygaard's ultimate demise would be but everything was shrouded in secrecy. He had great trust in Hawley though, which is why he signed for the part. He only suggested a rough character outline, which wasn't specific or detailed. It was just a general idea of where the writer wanted to go with the character. Hawley knew a great deal more than he was telling Freeman and he was careful with what was leaked out. Martin, therefore, did not have any particular clues as to what was coming in each episode. The cast were drip-fed the scripts when Hawley was ready to show them. As with many first-class writers, he did not want his actors to see the scripts until he, as the writer and creator, was a hundred-per-cent happy with them. Each script was, therefore, a surprise for Freeman and his fellow cast members. It also meant that nothing could be accidentally leaked to the public and thus potentially ruin the show's climax. Martin didn't know until past the halfway stage of filming the series what this would entail.

Freeman would read the script for, say, episode three and go, 'Wow, I didn't think that would happen,' and then read another episode script and think, 'Christ, I can't believe what's happened to…' The whole series was a surprise, which, in some respects, was easier for the actor because he didn't have to over-think or prepare too much and he could just be ready to move in whichever direction was necessary as the character moves on with each episode. It was all down to Hawley's command of the story as the writer and creator. By the end of the final episode Freeman was as surprised as anyone to see how Nygaard was capable of doing things that he had not been able to do at the start of the series.

However, Martin was initially dubious about taking on the role since he wondered – as he did with *Sherlock* – if there really needed to be a TV update of the original film. But then, of course, after reading the brilliant script, all initial reservations were debunked. He was quite vocal in correspondence with Noah Hawley that he did not want to be part of a *Fargo* tribute band. Hawley put his mind at rest and said that such a notion would not be the case. 'The fact that it uses a very famous and brilliant film as a jumping-off point was not really an attraction; you could have an appalling version of *Fargo*,' Freeman explained to *Vulture*'s Denise Martin. 'But this is a really, really good version! I can only go on the script that I'm sent, and this one was interesting, it was engaging, and it was surprising. I got to cover ground that I haven't covered before. I showed it to my missus and she's like, "You have to fuckin' do this." So I did.'

Freeman admired the work of the Coen Brothers from afar but said he had never been fanatical about them. He saw how the episode scripts tried to bring a sensibility to the films which was reminiscent of the Coen Brothers' best work. The brothers were only tangentially involved in the series but Freeman liked the fact that, in a sort of removed way, he was working with them. The series wouldn't have happened if they hadn't been involved. Martin was not interested in a literal remake – he liked that it echoes some of the traits of the original film but also brings a new sensibility to the story. The TV series stands on its own weight and does not rely on rehashing the original film. It inhabits the same world as the film but not the same characters, though it has the same darkly comic tone that the Coen Brothers excel at.

'Noah Hawley, who wrote all ten episodes, was definitely trying to tap into that,' Freeman told *The Observer*'s Andrew Anthony, 'and I think he did that successfully enough for them to give him their blessing. I don't know the Coen brothers but people I know who do say that's not easily won. But I had no interest in being in just a TV version of the film. As Billy Bob Thornton said, "If it was called Detroit, you'd still have to want to do it."'

Billy Bob Thornton has often come across as an enigmatic man, slightly odd and mercurial, but Freeman enjoyed working with him. He found Thornton to be a very easy and interesting actor to work with. They hit it off immediately, mostly talking about their shared love of music. Their first scene together was the emergency-room scene, which is the first time they meet on screen too. For Martin to work with such a distinguished and terrific actor was for him an absolute joy.

Some fans may recall that Billy Bob Thornton had a small role in *Love Actually* all those years ago.

'We'd never met on *Love Actually* but we got on instantly like a house on fire. As soon as we had our first line run it was apparent it was going to be a breeze,' Freeman enthused to BBC News website's Neil Smith. 'It's nice as well when you're working with an actor who you like watching. I was enjoying his performance as Martin, even as I was horrified by it as Lester.'

About their relationship on screen, Billy Bob Thornton explained to *Nerd Repository*'s Brent Hankins, 'We didn't really have to work on it. It just naturally happened. And Martin himself seems to be a very confident person, so I think he probably maybe had to downgrade his confidence a little bit. And me, by nature, I'm a very nervous, worrisome person, so I had to drop that a little. So, I think both of us had to definitely shed some of our real life stuff in order to play the characters.'

Both Freeman and Thornton share a similar belief that they are actors rather than movie stars. It is fascinating to watch the drama unfold between Nygaard and Malvo. As soon as they meet in the local hospital Malvo becomes a constant presence in Nygaard's life. Freeman did not get enough on-screen time with Thornton as he would have liked, as the characters' relationship develops sporadically throughout the series.

'All ten episodes are amazing,' Freeman expressed to *London Calling.com*'s Anthony Pearce. 'It's one of the best-written projects I've ever done. I wasn't interested in simply rehashing old territory. With *Fargo*, I feel we're covering ground that hadn't been covered in the film and stands on its own.'

Freeman did not, much to his disappointment, get to work with fellow co-star Colin Hanks, son of Tom. 'I really like him as a man, I'm very fond of him,' Martin admitted to *Nerd Repository*'s Kyle Wilson. 'And I've gotten to know him a little bit and he's a straight up lovely bloke. Yeah, I just really like him. And I did immediately. I think he's ever so good in the programme as well. I like his work a lot.'

One thing that Freeman did master, though it's somewhat odd, is his Minnesota accent. The actor has an acute musical ear and was able to pick up on the local dialect. He soon mastered the accent and stayed in voice all day on set.

'I'm having Skype lessons and, well, pride comes before a fall but I think I'm doing okay,' he said to *Time Out London*'s Nick Aveling. 'It's daunting. I don't want to rip off Bill Macy's accent, or rip off an accent that's already passed into comedy, so I've been on YouTube to see how real Minnesotans sound. Trouble is, some accents lend themselves to comedy. They just fucking do.'

Freeman takes on the role William H. Macy played in the original film. Ellen E. Jones of *The Independent* wrote of Freeman's performance, 'A Hampshire native, Freeman can't quite pull off the "Aw, jeez" Upper Midwest accent, which was such a joy in the original movie, and his befuddled nice-guy mannerisms are the same ones John Watson has in *Sherlock* and Tim had in *The Office*. He is so innately likable, in other words, he can't convey the snivelling self-interest which made William H. Macy's character compelling in the original. Or so it initially seemed.'

The British actor did not go back and watch the original film because he did not want it to interfere with his own vision for Nygaard.

'...as soon as you try and differ yourself from someone, you're becoming too conscious of that performance anyway,' Freeman told Anne Bayley of *TwoCentsTV.com*. 'So, no, I didn't feel pressure in that way... he's a brilliant actor and the world doesn't need another actor doing a Bill Macy impression and I don't need to be doing that and he doesn't need it and all of that. So, I purely treated it as my performance of a different character, albeit with some comparison. There are some parallels, but I was too busy concentrating on what I was doing with Lester really.'

Freeman was not immediately familiar with Mid-Western American culture so it was all a new experience for him. Middle America could have been Middle Earth for all he knew. He was trying to avoid a comic turn with his character and did not want to patronise Nygaard, which is what can happen when a character becomes endearing to the public.

'Every time that somebody comes up to me like that, like, "Oh, little baby,"... I'm a grown man,' Freeman said to *Vulture*'s Denise Martin. 'But the truth of some of those Minnesota accents is that even some Minnesotans think that they're kind of funny. So it's a fine line of getting that and honouring those characters. Not being reverential to them or patronising them, but to also acknowledge that some of the things the characters say are funny in the way that some of the things that are classically English are kind of ridiculous.'

He would have preferred to have spent time in the Mid-West pre-filming just to hang out in bars and coffee shops and speak to people to get a general gist of their way of life. Unfortunately, time did not permit him the opportunity. What Freeman did not want to do with the character was turn him into a caricature or a comedy figure of fun. Nor did he want to mock the Mid-Western way of life.

'I listened to a lot of Minnesotans, put it that way,' he said to *Nerd Repository*'s Kyle Wilson. 'That's why I didn't really go back and watch the initial film with *Fargo*, love it as I do, because I wanted to, for my research accent-wise, I wanted it to be actual Minnesotans and not actors playing Minnesotans. Any more than I would expect an actor who wants to play a Minnesotan to study me. They shouldn't study me, they should study a Minnesotan.'

Freeman was hoping that playing such a role would dispel the notion that he is only able to play nice men. By accepting the part, he was challenging people's perceptions of him as well as challenging himself and his own body of work.

'I'm under no illusion about what I appear like,' he told *The Observer*'s Andrew Anthony. 'I just know there's more to me than that as a person, and there's certainly more to me than that as an actor. That's where the frustration comes. My plan was always to be an actor. It wasn't to be a nice guy. I became famous in Britain playing a nice decent guy and that casts a long shadow.'

Lester Nygaard does not start off as a bad guy; he's a normal, very average middle-of-the-road man whose bad-guy persona develops as the story progresses, much like *Breaking Bad*'s Walter White.

'When I read the script I thought, ooh, that's quite Walter White-ish. But where Lester Nygaard starts off with you sympathising with him, and everything he does is understandable, Richard just starts off going: I am a cunt, and here's why I'm a cunt…,' Freeman said to the *Daily Telegraph*'s Craig McLean. 'He's revelling in it. Whereas Lester would never consider himself a tosser. Like most people don't.'

The frustration and the pent-up anger that is in Lester Nygaard is inside everyone. Everyone has moments where they want to throw something out of the window or hit someone in a split second. But there is a barrier between thinking about something and actually carrying out the proposed act. For Nygaard, that barrier breaks down when he kills his own wife. His thoughts and actions become one. He regrets it but, throughout the series, he also feels liberated by it and cannot stop himself from doing awful things. Nygaard's world is shaken after murdering his wife and he doesn't know how to react because he has never acted on emotions before. He then spends his time thinking about how the outside world will react to her murder and so he thinks of how he can get away with it and convince people that he is sad that his wife was murdered, because, of course, the killer, in the eyes of the locals, remains at large. He tries to act upset because the locals think such a devastated husband could not have killed his wife. It takes him time to work on that persona of his, which is ultimately all fake. He becomes more of a man as the series progresses but only in the sense that he makes up his own mind and governs his own life based on his own thoughts and feelings rather than the feelings of others: people that bullied him into doing things and those who called him weak for not fending for himself. However, Nygaard soon learns that he cannot control his life anymore as his actions spiral out of control.

'I think Lester is pretty universal. There are Lesters everywhere in every race and walk of life and country,' Freeman explained to *Nerd Repository*'s Kyle Wilson. 'There are people who are sort of downtrodden and people who are under-confident and all that, so that was more a case of tapping into that in myself really.'

People don't think of Martin as the type who plays a murderer so the challenge made a refreshing change from his comedic and dramatic roles of the past. The change in Lester's character was, in part, an attraction that Freeman found alluring.

'I just loved it. I've said to my agents for ages in a kind of lighthearted way that I think I need to play a serial killer, a fucking rapist, drug dealer, whatever,' he admitted to *TVGuide*'s Hanh Nguyen. 'Partly because people don't see me like that and partly because I want to flex those muscles again. Before *The Office*, I was a young actor in London who casting agents saw as kind of edgy. I would be going up for those parts that were a bit violent or a bit scuzzy.'

Freeman was once in the running to play the villain in Peter Jackson's 2007 adaptation of the best-selling Alice Sebold novel, *The Lovely Bones*. His *Sherlock* co-star Benedict Cumberbatch has recently carved out a career as a successful villain, with roles as Kahn in *Star Trek* and Smaug in *The Hobbit*. Freeman has always wanted to play more roles and, though he is not a villain as such in *Fargo*, there is something worrying and sinister about his character: a hapless, sad, everyday middle-class American who gets trodden on by everyone in his life until he meets Billy Bob Thornton's character.

'Yes, if there is any plan ever it's to play as much as possible,' he said on the idea of playing darker roles to *GQ*'s Oliver Franklin. 'Not to big myself up too much, I think I play a lot within a second, do you know what I mean? You're not saying I am, but if I was someone who was playing one thing all the time, that would be something else. But I think I'm quite capable of bringing out colour and shade in any character.'

The freezing-cold temperatures of Calgary certainly helped Freeman develop his character. And, of course, he missed his family enormously. Calgary was the coldest place Martin had ever been to in his life, with temperatures dropping as low as twelve degrees below freezing. The UK may have a reputation for being cold and dreary but it is Hawaii compared to Calgary. Even on mild days it was considerably colder than London. It was a bit of a culture shock for Freeman. His surroundings helped him focus on the script and to learn more about his character, to develop Nygaard's mannerisms, but all the hard work was really down to Noah Hawley, who had the character developed to a T.

'It's very apparent by the end of the first episode that this is not all that meets the eye,' he said to Daniel Fienberg of *Hitfix*. 'So I thought, "Well, geez, if that happens at the end of the first episode, what the hell is Episode Ten gonna be?" So that was the thing that gave me confidence that I would be fully engaged and fully interested in what I was doing. And I have been! Every script I've read has just been better and better and better. It's been fantastic.'

He was shocked at the breakneck speed at which each episode episode was made – he was not used to that sort of fast-paced environment. It was a good experience for him and any ideas that he had, had to be brought to the forefront straight away, before the cameras were set up for the next shot.

Though everyone came from different backgrounds, he found them all to be professional and very easy to work with. The cast turned up on time, read their lines and got on with the job at hand without ego or fuss. There was much mutual respect and no frivolous off-screen performances or anything equally immature. It was all very professional. Everyone involved knew they were making something rather superlative.

There is a dark humour to *Fargo* and with a background in both comedy and drama, Freeman knew exactly how to approach his character. He knew there can be comedy in anything serious, so long as it is handled wisely.

'*The Sopranos* sometimes really makes me laugh and that's not a comedy,' he said to *Nerd Repository*'s Kyle Wilson. 'And sometimes I'm almost crying at the pathos of Laurel and Hardy, which is not a drama. So, I believe in both of those things being there and I don't think it's a big deal by both things being there. So, when Lester has moments of comedy as there are in the show, yes, I think, you know, without blowing my own trumpet, I think I can do it. And I think I'm not bad at it, so, yeah, all of that I think it doesn't hurt. I think it all helps stir the pot somehow, yeah.'

The series won the cast and crew rave reviews.

'Of course, *Fargo* also functions as a crime thriller but there was a narrative drive amid the madness,' wrote the *Daily Telegraph*'s Ben Lawrence of the first episode. 'The scene in which Nygaard battered his crowing wife to death with a hammer and was confronted by Thurman, who then gets it in the back from Malvo, was grimly compelling. But the mood was lightened by Freeman's performance. His air of nervy bewilderment recalled his sitcom roles, as if Tim from *The Office* had stumbled into the house of Atreus.'

Entertainment Weekly's Karen Valby wrote, 'Poor, angry, pent-up Lester, henpecked by everyone – Freeman brings a taut energy to the character. (After committing an evil act in the pilot, Lester frantically calls Lorne's motel room for guidance. "Yeah, it's me, you got to help me, I've done something bad," he squawks into the phone. "Leroy Motor Inn?" the front-desk receptionist says. Lester: "Oh, hi, room 23, please.") Freeman's Lester is the perfect bumbling counterpart to Thornton's graceful Lorne, whose look and demeanour seem a direct descendant of Javier Bardem's Anton Chigurh.'

Writing in *USA Today*, Robert Bianco said, 'Oh, and in Billy Bob Thornton and Martin Freeman, it has a pair of stars whose brilliantly written and played dynamic gives the warped relationship between Matthew McConaughey and Woody Harrelson in *True Detective* a run for its money.'

He continued to say, 'And through it all, there's the riveting performances of Thornton and Freeman. Wait for the way Thornton can shift from a sly smile to a venomous gaze, or the way Freeman mixes Lester's frustration, fear and regret with flashes of relief.'

Freeman is not a careerist as such, though he now joins fellow Brits Andrew Lincoln and Jonny Lee Miller, who are currently starring in successful American TV shows and have become near-enough household names stateside. However, what has always turned Martin away from American TV is the lengthy multiple-season contracts that the actors have to sign. He does not seem to play the actor's game and there is something very British about Martin Freeman. *Fargo* appealed to him because, like *True Detective*, it is an anthology series so Freeman only had to sign up for one season.

'I'm an actor, I want to play good parts and it's a good part,' he said to *Hitfix*'s Daniel Fienberg. 'There are a couple of fantastic scenes with Lorne Malvo, Billy Bob's character, that really keep me in the story and the potential for where this character might go and what his story might be. I felt like I had very little choice [he laughs], given that it was also finite. It wasn't going on for six years. It was ten episodes, several months. That was pretty cool for me.'

The difficult aspect of a TV series that writers face is the conclusion. There is nothing more devastating for a committed viewer and loyal fan to watch countless hours of a TV series only to witness an anticlimax, as evidence by *True Blood*, the HBO vampire series. Some series run out of steam so that you no longer care about the characters or the story, in which case a disappointing end does not feel like a cheat, but you only see it if you've stuck with it, and not chosen to watch something else.

Fargo season one is just about the right amount of episodes, with some wonderful, albeit dark, characters and some intriguing plot twists that keep you hooked. But what of the ending? Naturally – as with any revered series (and even the ending of highly-lauded *True Detective* was met with negative criticism, as was *Breaking Bad* from some quarters of its fan base, though the writers of any series cannot please everyone) – *Fargo* did not impress everyone but it managed to both surprise and satisfy. Thankfully, fans did not feel cheated, as they did with *Lost* or *Dexter* – this latter brilliant serial-killer drama delivered possibly the most unsatisfactory and embarrassing finale in modern American television.

In Michael Hogan's rave review of the episode titled 'Morton's Fork' in the *Daily Telegraph*, he praised the final episode: 'All the storylines were satisfactorily tied up, so even after ten weeks of death and darkness, we still got that rarest of things in modern drama: a happy ending. And a moral one.'

What makes *Fargo* such a compelling story is not only the outstanding writing but the two lead characters – Lester Nygaard and Lorne Malvo, both of whom are rather likeable despite the many misgivings we have about them and their repugnant acts of evil.

'He never stops being human, you know?' Freeman expressed to *Hitfix*'s Daniel Fienberg. 'But in a funny way, neither does Billy Bob's character. He is always human, too. That's the beauty of good writing and good casting. Even someone as truly dark as Lorne Malvo is still very attractive and you want to spend time with him, because he's a fun character.'

Fargo stands as one of the finest TV dramas of the decade, along with such masterful creations as *Breaking Bad* and *Hannibal*. *Fargo* was another impeccable piece of television writing that possibly exceeds *Sherlock*, with numerous twists and turns in the plot as the first series reaches a nail-biting conclusion.

Freeman began 2015 with the BBC broadcast of the highly-acclaimed TV film *The Eichmann Show*, as part of the BBC's Holocaust memorial season. The film portrays the story of the blacklisted television director Leo Hurwitz (played by Aussie actor Anthony LaPaglia) and the 1961 trial of Nazi war criminal Adolf Eichmann. Eichmann was apprehended in Argentina in 1960 and, as the chief architect of the Holocaust, went to trial in Israel the following year. The footage of the trial was shown on TV in thirty-seven countries. Freeman stars as producer Milton Fruchtman who spearheaded the project. The film delicately intercuts real-life archive footage with dramatized scenes. TV pundits praised the film with *The Observer*'s Euan Ferguson calling it a 'phenomenal retelling'.

'Because as the best television gets more and more what we would call filmic,' Freeman said to *Nerd Repository*'s Kyle Wilson, 'and a lot of the best writing I think has been pretty much acknowledged for ten years has been on television, I think there's much less of a differentiation now than there was maybe twenty, thirty years ago. And so I don't have a preference.'

Fargo challenged people's perception of Freeman as an actor, showing film and TV followers that he is more than capable of playing edgy characters. It was a wise career move and one that will no doubt pay dividends, especially in the US where he remains best known for *The Office*, *The Hobbit* and *Sherlock*. In June 2014 Billy Bob Thornton picked up the Best Actor In A Mini-Series Or Movie award at the fourth annual Television Critics' Association Awards, beating his co-star Martin Freeman. Allison Tolman, their co-star, scooped the Best Supporting Actress In A Mini-Series Or Movie award. Freeman's other show, *Sherlock*, went home empty-handed despite several nominations.

The 2014 Emmy Awards nominations were announced in

July, which featured some well-known British names, including Martin Freeman. *Fargo* picked up a staggering eighteen nods, including nominations for its two lead stars, while Freeman also bagged a second nomination in the Best Supporting Actor In A Mini-Series Or Movie category for 'His Last Vow'.

The 2014 Emmy Awards took place in Los Angeles on Monday, 25 April. Freeman and his fellow *Sherlock* actor Benedict Cumberbatch were not at the ceremony to collect their awards for Best Supporting Actor and Best Actor In A Mini-Series. Steven Moffat also won Best Writing In A Mini-Series for the final episode of the third season of *Sherlock*. There were four awards for the universally acclaimed BBC series, including Best Cinematography, Music, Single-Camera Picture Editing and Sound Editing.

'It's great to see *Sherlock* being recognised so spectacularly at the Emmys,' said Ben Stephenson, controller of BBC drama. 'I'm delighted that the BBC is home to so much world class acting and writing talent.'

Freeman's other TV series, *Fargo*, bagged the award for Best Mini-Series.

It was announced in mid-2014 that Freeman, Billy Bob Thornton, Colin Hanks and Allison Tolman would not be returning for the second series of *Fargo* due to air in late 2015 at the earliest. Noah Hawley was confirmed to continue as writer and executive producer but there'll be a new storyline and time period spread over ten episodes. As with *True Detective*, *Fargo* will be an anthology series, which recalls the old pulp-story anthologies of the immediate post-World War II era. There's no question that Freeman fans were disappointed by the news.

Some fans always feel cheated with anthology series because they get so close to the characters that, by the end of the season, they're left wanting more, but the end is the end. Will viewers return for a second season? Will the scripts and actors be as good as season one? Vintage anthology series such as *The Outer Limits* and *The Twilight Zone* have had a massive impact on science-fiction and fantasy and *American Horror Story* is a successful contemporary anthology series that has run for four seasons with the possibility of a fifth (at the time of writing) but, mostly, anthology series don't have much of an impact, especially in an age of multiple channels, the Internet, downloading and streaming.

On the positive side, it meant that Freeman was free to move on to other roles. He is not an actor who likes to be tied down to projects for long periods of time, though *Sherlock* and *The Hobbit* are two obvious exceptions. He signed onto *Fargo* knowing there would be no more than the ten-episode first series.

Hawley dropped hints to *The Hollywood Reporter* about the possible concepts for season two: 'I feel like I'm close to a new idea for another *Fargo* ten-hour idea that we'll talk about in the coming weeks… What's really interesting about this exercise of emulating a movie, as a storyteller, is having available to me a whole body of work. The Coen Brothers are so varied, from *Raising Arizona* to *A Serious Man* – there's so much… What is the inspiration for this season? It's always going to be rooted in true crime. There will always be a grisly murder, with good versus evil.'

Just as Matthew McConaughey can sit back and enjoy season two of *True Detective* as an ordinary viewer, Freeman will no doubt enjoy watching *Fargo* season two when it broadcasts on TV, and may even pick up the box set for his ever-growing collection of DVDs. Martin had moved on to the stage in his career where he could pick and choose, quite literally, which roles he wanted to play. The scripts were coming in left, right and centre and his US and UK agents were busy on the phone negotiating new contracts and roles. He also has the opportunity to pick roles that will pay much less than he is ordinarily used to without having to worry about not being able to support his family and paying the bills.

Freeman made a return to the London stage with a production of *Richard III* in the summer of 2014 at Trafalgar Studios. His *Hobbit* colleague Richard Armitage was at The Old Vic starring in *The Crucible*, the acclaimed Arthur Miller play.

'… that's a pretty iconic role and that's one I'm very happy about,' he said to *ShortList.com* about being cast as Richard III. 'I wasn't expecting that and I didn't see it coming, so when that came, director Jamie Lloyd asked me to do that – I was very pleasantly surprised to be asked to do that, and one that I grabbed with both hands.

It was Freeman's first theatre role since the Pulitzer Prize-winning *Clybourne Park*, directed by Dominic Cooke at the Royal Court four years earlier, but he was more than pleased to be back on stage starring opposite *The Borgias* actress Gina McKee. Additional casting includes Alasdair Buchan (Ensemble – an ensemble cast is made up of cast members in which the principle actors and performers are assigned roughly equal amounts of importance and screen time in a production), Simon Coombs (Tyrrel), Philip Cumbus (Richmond),

Madeleine Harland (Ensemble), Julie Jupp (Ensemble), Gerald Kyd (Catesby), Joshua Lacey (Rivers), Paul Leonard (Stanley), Gabrielle Lloyd (Duchess of York), Forbes Masson (Hastings), Paul McEwan (King Edward IV/Bishop of Ely), Mark Meadows (Clarence/Lord Mayor), Vinta Morgan (Edward of Lancaster/ Ensemble), Lauren O'Neil (Lady Anne), Maggie Steed (Queen Margaret) and Jo Stone-Fewings (Buckingham).

Freeman feels very comfortable in theatre. However, the deformed Machiavellian regent was his first stab at a professional Shakespeare production, much to the surprise of some people given his background in theatre and TV.

'There have been amateurish-in-drama-school ones,' he informed the *Daily Telegraph*'s Craig McLean. 'But yeah, I can't believe it – I've been out of drama school nineteen years, and this is the first time I've done it professionally. I'm surprised.'

Martin has always had an interest in the Bard's plays on a professional level, as he said back in 2005 when he spoke to *The Globe And Mail*'s Simon Houpt: 'I'd love to play Macbeth. See, the thing is, what I think I can do and what the perception of what I can do – there's quite a gulf between the two, because obviously people don't know my work. But I do. Probably no one would think I'd make a good Macbeth, but I know I would.'

Richard III was directed by Jamie Lloyd. He had also directed James McAvoy in a production of *Macbeth* but, whereas *Macbeth* was set in a future dystopia, *Richard III* is 'an imaginary dystopia from a few decades ago. Twentieth century,' as Freeman described it to Craig McLean of *The Telegraph*.

'When I first met Jamie he asked if I'd seen this documentary about this political event in our British history,' he continued.

The official press release for *Richard III* described the play thus: 'In the aftermath of civil war, Richard, Duke of Gloucester, makes a hateful resolution to claw his way to political power at any cost. A master of manipulation, subtle wit and beguiling charm, he orchestrates his unlawful ascent by spinning a ruthless web of deceit and betrayal. His staunch ambition soon begins to weigh heavy, as the new ruler finds himself utterly alone and steeped in dread, forced to answer for his bloody deeds and face the horrifying consequences.'

Lloyd's *Macbeth* made tough viewing for members of the audience but Freeman shared a similar vision with Lloyd that they are totally against making people bored in the theatre, which makes *Richard III* rather more difficult as it is the second lengthiest work in the playwright's hefty catalogue of plays. They made sure that the physical deformities – malformed arm, limp and hunchback – were all there, which has a major effect on his view of the world, and Freeman, as Richard III, begins the production by telling the audience he's not a nice person and he's going to plot and scheme because of the way he's been treated due to his deformities. Characters' actions have to be justifiable. There is a reason why bad people do bad things. Freeman even made remarks to the effect that the character of Richard III is much like Gollum from *The Hobbit*.

Freeman made damn sure that his version of Richard III was as far away as possible from his own likeable, everyday persona. Indeed, with *Fargo* and *Richard III*, it's almost as if Martin is undergoing a professional career makeover.

'When you get known for something, you get a few more of those roles and before you know it you're in people's consciousness as that thing,' Freeman told Neil Smith of the BBC News website. 'But I'm not just that optimistic, nice person or mild-mannered sweetheart next door. So it's nice when people see something in me that isn't *Love Actually*.'

However, it was reported during the play's previews in the first week of July that over-eager younger fans of *The Hobbit* were ruining the play by clapping and cheering at inappropriate times.

Claire Dikecoglu, a well-known Arts blogger, said, 'I was irritated when the audience interrupted the flow of the play to clap and cheer Martin's first scene. I understand that Martin Freeman is popular, but I have no bigger pet peeve, than everything getting standing ovations these days.'

'Martin Freeman's face is on every bus in London,' said actress Maureen Lipman, as referenced in *The Independent*. 'The producers are aiming for people who spend most of their day with wire in their ears. It is not so much Richard III as Richard the rock concert.'

On Twitter, the director Jamie Lloyd said, 'A few people clapped after the first scene during the first preview. It is not unusual for an audience to clap during scene changes...' and, 'It has never happened since and has been completely overblown. Ridiculous. The standing ovations have been instant & from young & old alike.'

This was a refreshing role for Freeman that not only challenged him as an actor but, much like his recent choices in film and TV roles, challenged audiences' perceptions of him as the dreaded and now clichéd 'everyman'. There must come a point where people no longer see him that way.

Professional theatre critics gave the play mixed to positive reviews but praised Freeman, though many found the play to be complicated. The set from award-winning designer Soutra Gilmour was also highly praised.

Critics appeared to share a similar mindset that, while Freeman has a much-deserved reputation for his sometimes quirky yet interesting approaches to texts due to his impeccable comic timing and underlying anger, his performance as Richard III all comes down to how the viewer interprets Richard III in the play, regardless of who the actor is. Some prefer Richard III to be played as a brooding man who has boundless amounts of charisma, yet he is someone who is sickening and repulsive at the same time. He is also amusing.

Michael Billington of *The Guardian* wrote, 'It's fair to say that Freeman's Richard is perfectly suited to the concept. This is no grandiose villain but a dapper, smooth-haired figure who only gradually reveals his psychopathic tendencies.'

Paul Taylor of *The Independent* enthused, 'Freeman gives a highly intelligent, calculatedly understated performance, full of witty mocking touches in his rapid line-readings (he refers to 'this princely... heap' with a comically fastidious pause) and creating a rapport of shared superiority with the audience over his dupes.'

Ben Brantley of the *New York Times* wrote, 'What he lacks is that hypnotic force of will that allows Richard to seduce a country, not to mention women like the doomed Lady Anne (Lauren O'Neil). It seems fitting that a later potential conquest,

Elizabeth (Gina McKee), will listen to Richard's suit only after she's been trussed up in a chair by his henchman.'

Meanwhile, Charles Spencer of the *Daily Telegraph* wrote, 'As the evil Richard, Freeman seems frankly miscast. The great trick of the play is that Richard seduces the audience with his wit and panache, even as he leads us into a moral wasteland of cruel barbarity. Compared with the great Richards I have seen over the years – Antony Sher, Ian McKellen, Simon Russell Beale and Kevin Spacey – Freeman seems like a boy sent to do a man's work.'

Henry Hitchings of the *London Evening Standard* observed, 'Martin Freeman is a smiling, self-satisfied Richard III – not the psychopath we tend to see, but instead an illustration of the banality of evil. He makes the hunchbacked monarch efficient and dapper, rather like a prim bureaucrat. Yet he punctuates this ordinariness with moments of malign mockery and savagery. It's a crisp, thoughtful performance, in which Freeman successfully shakes off his familiar Nice Guy image. But he never seems truly dangerous.'

It is not unusual for high-profile actors to receive criticism in the theatre. It is part and parcel of the job. However, it was actually Freeman's intention to bring Shakespeare to younger audiences, as he told Andrew Marr on his TV show that he wanted to cut out the 'boring bits'. He said, 'Among very educated, very smart, very theatre-literate people who sort of tolerate the boring bits and boring passages without telling anybody and tolerate the bits of the play where they think, "I don't know who she is," and, "Who's he talking to?" without saying so because that would sort of be a black mark against them.'

Some theatregoers and critics may find his remarks patronising but there is something noble about wanting to entice younger people to the theatre. The play's website stated that only people over twelve should see the show. As quoted in the *Daily Mail*, Chris McGovern, chairman of the Campaign for Real Education, rebutted, 'I don't think children should get some diluted version, it's very patronising and it means they will never understand what drama is about.' He continued, 'But [Mr Freeman's] view isn't unusual, it's very prevalent within schools, the idea that children can't cope and that it has to be watered down… I think it's very anti-educational and very patronising and it deprives children of an understanding of what a play is all about.'

However, and despite the minor controversy, Freeman was applauded by audience members as many fans posted rave reviews of his performance on Twitter. Such is the age we live in that social media is awash with instant reviews, headlines and newsbytes. Fans used to have to wait for the newspaper or magazine reviews, which could take days or weeks, but in the twenty-first century everything is instant.

While Freeman was on the London stage until September and Cumberbatch was busy with multiple movies and a move to the theatre with a production of Hamlet at the Barbican, it meant that series four of *Sherlock* could not be filmed in the autumn as originally hoped, and so the schedule was put back to begin in January 2015.

Freeman told the *Sunday Telegraph*'s *Seven* magazine, 'If that's going to be a special – I'm speaking off-message here; if this was New Labour I'd get fired – I think that might be for next Christmas. A Christmas special. That's what I understand.'

It was then confirmed by the BBC that *Sherlock* series four would be broadcast in late 2015 with a one-off special. In the same interview, Freeman also said that his partner is likely to return: 'While we play fast and loose with the original stories, we generally follow the trajectory of what Conan Doyle did. So he [Watson] gets married, and then Mary dies – so at some point presumably she'll die.'

In the original Conan Doyle stories, Mary Morstan dies sometime during the period between Holmes's apparent death at the Reichenbach Falls and his shocking return three years later. However, both of these events have already taken place in *Sherlock*. In the stories, Mary dies of natural causes but it is likely she will meet her demise in a far more adventurous fashion in the series, given that she is a former assassin. Watson picks up the pieces and joins Holmes in more adventures, which opens up the possibility of more one-off specials or even a fifth series but Freeman is likely to be in the frame of mind that the fourth series should be the last. A twelve-episode, four-series run is perfect and will have the sort of longevity afforded to all the great long-running TV shows.

Freeman told BBC News in August 2014, 'It's going to be full of surprises for you, and for us and for everybody. I think we just know to expect the unexpected now.' He added, 'The plans they have got for the overarching series – oh man, it's just so exciting!'

In a sense, Moffat and Gatiss, the creators of the modern-day *Sherlock*, are living on borrowed time. The Hollywood careers of Cumberbatch and Freeman are doing so well that it is unlikely they will want to keep going back to the BBC regardless of how loyal they are to the small-screen show. It's not about ego but rather the logistics of making a TV show – regardless of its global popularity – around so many Hollywood movies. Perhaps there is also the question of money because, usually, the more successful an actor is, the more expensive he becomes. Of course, actors take salary cuts but Hollywood is fickle – as is the entertainment industry in general – and an actor's success tends to be based on his financial worth. An actor who makes millions is generally considered to be very popular. It's doubtful that both of the *Sherlock* protagonists will stray too far from their London acting roots though.

Moffat said at the Ad-Lib event at the Edinburgh Fringe Festival, 'The show could not continue without Benedict and Martin. It's absolutely them… Benedict and Martin have been announcing on various red carpets that they're happy to come back and keep doing it. It would be quite nice to do it for a long, long time – let them age and become the normal aged Sherlock Holmes and Doctor Watson.'

However, co-creator Steven Moffat also admitted that, if they were to do long runs of *Sherlock*, they would lose Cumberbatch and Freeman to Hollywood and that many more series of the BBC1 drama would not be possible.

Moffat spoke to *EntertainmentWise.com* at the premier of the Marvel movie, *Guardians of the Galaxy*, which stars former *Doctor Who* actor Karen Gillan: 'It's because it's an occasional treat, every two years you get back together and make a few of them and that can go on for a bit… We're all very excited by it and we all support whatever other successes we have or are having.'

Freeman has had an extraordinary career with so many varying roles to his name. As with all the great actors, he's been in some garbage but his performances always shine. For him to jump from a major Hollywood movie to a British TV show to a Shakespearean play is evidence of just how talented he is. He's also an actor who will not settle; he is constantly challenging himself. It's a journey he has been on since his teenage years when he decided that he wanted to become an actor. He's starred in thrillers, dramas, comedy, fantasy and Shakespeare. You name it, he can do it. And while he detests being labelled an 'everyman', there is much to like about Freeman as an actor. Being an 'everyman' is not a bad thing, of course. James Stewart, Jack Lemmon and Tom Hanks made careers out of their everyday, accessible and friendly personas.

'You don't see people like me walking up and down the street,' he said to *Esquire*'s Michael Holden. 'You don't, frankly, see this [he points to his jacket] all the time and I'm not trying to give myself the big thing but you don't. Not everyone dresses like me. Not everyone has my record collection because that implies I'm beige and I'm not fucking beige, you know. That's the headline isn't it?'

Freeman entered the acting profession out of a desire for joy and play and because it is something he happens to be very good at. It's very upsetting if people don't like him, as it is with anything, but he is the ultimate critic of his work. He knows when he has given a good performance or not. There are many things in life he finds daunting but work is not one of them. He does not worry about work; he enjoys it even when it frustrates the hell out of him.

'It's not something I was ever seeking and of course I understand that it's the nature of this business, that with success comes recognition,' he told Anthony Pearce of *London Calling.com*. 'It can be pleasant to have people acknowledge your work and express their appreciation but sometimes the attention can be difficult to bear, and I admit I'm not good at that sort of thing. I like having my little world to myself and for my friends and family.'

Acting certainly does have its pitfalls but there is nothing else Freeman would rather be doing. He has moments where he questions his profession and he does get bad days on set, just like anybody gets with any job, but he loves his work. What brings out the best in him is when he is working with other people. He gets to meet a whole boatload of new people with every job, some of whom he manages to work with on more than one project. Acting is just about the best way to earn a living as far as Freeman is concerned.

'Sometimes it's hard to say. It's like being in love or loving people,' he told Anne Bayley of *TwoCentsTV.com*. 'If you really sort of say, but what do I love about that person? Sometimes you've actually got to sit down and think, hang on, do I love them or is this habit or whatever, you know? So, you've got to kind of think for a minute about whether you do still love something. And I do that with acting.'

Freeman is not an actor that you will read about in the paper immersing himself in some sort of hedonistic lifestyle, the kind of behaviour that is often popularised by the tabloid press. It's probably very frustrating for the salacious end of the journalistic spectrum that Freeman is a pretty ordinary, casual guy. There's no dirt to be dug up, no stories of extramarital affairs – he's totally committed to his wife and children. Nor is he especially adventurous.

'Well, depending on the adventure. I mean I wouldn't go into life-and-death [situations] really but nor would anyone unless you're a moron,' he told the *New Zealand Herald*. He continued, 'But I'm an actor and I've chosen a life where there's no security, where there's no wages, no pension – so for a start that's braver than those who go to work at the bank in my opinion.'

CHAPTER TEN

THE FINAL ADVENTURE
IN MIDDLE EARTH

2 014 closed with the release of the third and final *Hobbit* film, *The Hobbit: The Battle of the Five Armies* on 12 December, following in the footsteps of *The Hobbit: An Unexpected Journey* (2012) and *The Hobbit: The Desolation of Smaug* (2013). The third film had been confirmed on 30 July 2012 after the creative team chose to extend the story from the original two-film idea. *The Battle of the Five Armies* expands the story of Middle Earth as Tolkien described in the appendices to *The Return of the King*.

Director Peter Jackson announced that the film would use footage already shot but not used in the first two films as well as additional material. The original title was *There and Back Again* but it was later changed to *The Battle of the Five Armies* in April 2014. Jackson stated on his Facebook page that he felt the new title was better suited to the story and that *There and*

Back Again would have been better for the second film in a two-film story but not for the final film in the trilogy.

'I didn't find it hard,' Freeman said to *Hollywood Reporter*'s Jordan Zakarin about completing filming. 'I think the hardest part about anything you do for eighteen months is just keeping yourself together for eighteen months. But I do think I'm quite good casting for it. I don't think I'm the only one, but as a candidate, I think I was pretty good casting.'

The trailer for *The Battle of the Five Armies* was premiered at Comic-Con in San Diego in July. Freeman could not attend the event as he was starring in *Richard III* in London.

Cumberbatch spoke about the film at Comic-Con. He told the audience, 'I think rather like *The Lord of the Rings* there is obviously a natural progression to the end and that means it will be a pinnacle of sorts, it will top what's come before it. It's about building to this point so as far as the end of the story goes I think it will be the greatest of the three to be seen so far, for obvious, narrative reasons.'

Fans were coming round to the idea that there will be no more Middle Earth adventures, at least from Peter Jackson. Cumberbatch added, 'That to me already sort of heightens the enormity of what it is going to be as an experience as a filmgoer. But I am kind of in the dark – I don't do all that much in this film, and there is a hell of a lot that is done in this film so I am going to be equally surprised and fascinated when I see it all.'

Freeman realises that he'll forever be remembered as Bilbo Baggins, just as Mark Hamill is remembered for Luke Skywalker, Harrison Ford as Indiana Jones and Christian Bale as Batman in *Batman: The Dark Knight*.

'I hope by the time my life is over I've given them something else to talk about,' he continued to tell Zakarin of the franchise's relentless fandom, 'but I think in all reality I think it's very likely that they'll be calling me Bilbo.'

The Lord of the Rings actor Viggo Mortensen criticised Jackson ('I guess Peter became like Ridley Scott – this one-man industry now, with all these people depending on him') and the trilogy of films in an interview with the *Daily Telegraph*'s Tom Robey in May: '… really the second and third ones were a mess. It was very sloppy – it just wasn't done at all. It needed massive reshoots, which we did, year after year. But he would have never been given the extra money to do those if the first one hadn't been a huge success. The second and third ones would have been straight to video.'

It can certainly be argued that *The Hobbit* films rely on style over substance and Peter Jackson would not be the first director to become obsessed with technology over basic storytelling techniques such as plot, characters and dialogue.

Freeman's rebuttal to the *Daily Telegraph*'s Craig McLean was, 'All I can say is: I hope that's not the case. I know Peter and the team who make those films, they'd be horrified to think they'd jettisoned all subtlety. Yeah, there's a lot of CGI, an awful lot of that business going on. But they are still very, very interested in story. They want the human side of it to be absolutely pivotal. Beyond that? Of course it's a question of taste and I respect Viggo's opinion.'

The film sees the dwarves find and wake the dragon Smaug while the battle between the goblins and the wargs, the men of Lake Town, the elves, the dwarves, the eagles and Beorn takes place as they attempt to gain control of The Lonely Mountain (Erebor) and the treasure that lies inside it.

The film stars Martin Freeman and Ian Holm as Bilbo Baggins as well as Cate Blanchett as Galadriel, Benedict Cumberbatch as Smaug/Necromancer, Evangeline Lilly as Tauriel, Manu Bennett as Azog, Richard Armitage as Thorin Oakenshield, Lee Pace as Thranduil, Orlando Bloom as Legolas, Luke Evans as Bard, Ian McKellen as Gandalf, Hugo Weaving as Elrond, Christopher Lee as Saruman, Billy Connolly as Dáin, Mikael Persbrandt as Beorn and Graham McTavish as Dwalin. Joining them is Ken Stott, Aidan Turner, Dean O'Gorman, Mark Hadlow, Jed Brophy, Adam Brown, John Callen, Peter Hambleton, William Kircher, James Nesbitt, Stephen Hunter, Bret McKenzie, Ryan Gage, Sylvester McCoy, Lawrence Makoare, John Bell, Simon London and Robin Kerr.

'He's incredibly moving in the third film and that's always surprising because you think you know Martin to be a great comedian but he's also a great dramatic actor as well,' Richard Armitage (who plays Thorin Oakenshield) said to the *Radio Times*'s Susanna Lazarus. 'I really enjoyed working with him and I think a lot of the evolution of Thorin is down to the way that he portrayed Bilbo. There wouldn't be a Thorin without a Bilbo.'

What an adventure Bilbo Baggins has been on, and so has Martin Freeman. The actor spoke to *Flicks And Bits* about his character's heroic journey and representation of himself as the audience have watched Bilbo Baggins become a hero: 'I think like with any real-life heroics, no hero considers themselves a hero. You speak to people in the fire service or the military or whatever and they don't see what they're doing as heroic at all.

And with Bilbo it's heroism that kind of creeps up on him, out of necessity – because he's got to save his friends' lives or he's got to save his own life, so it's fight or flight.'

Freeman saw something of a resemblance between the life of a hobbit (an insulated though rather cosy world of drinking tea and staying at home) and that of a typical middle-aged English person.

'... it's easy to say because I am English, you know?' Freeman said to *MSN Entertainment*'s James Rocchi. 'Maybe if I was American then... but there's something also very American about not going abroad isn't there? I think it's fairly human. I think it's fairly universal. It feels English because Tolkien is English and because I'm English I sound English. But I think you could probably apply it to most cultures that there is a love of home. There is a love of your homeland and sometimes a reluctance to leaving it for very long.'

The films had taken some criticism from fans and reviewers who attacked them for being overlong and overblown and an exaggeration of the original novel but they were a major stepping stone towards gaining Martin Freeman mainstream prominence and recognition in Hollywood. *The Hobbit* trilogy may not stand as highly respected as *The Lord of the Rings* trilogy but they are high-quality fantasy films. *The Hobbit: The Battle of the Five Armies* will surely smash box-office records.

The final piece in the story sees this once meek and timid character turned into an extraordinary hero.

'You spend so much time playing Bilbo as this reticent person who is just trying to find his voice and trying to find when to speak,' Freeman said to *AsiaOne*, 'just finding permission to breathe almost, that it is really good fun in this film when he does have to find that bit of steel inside himself. He really, really has to find that for his own safety and that of his friends.'

Though Freeman never had a specific life plan as far as acting was concerned, he knew he didn't want to sell out to Hollywood glitz and glamour as well as to all the dodgy run-of-the-mill screenplays. Early in his career he had overly developed feelings against selling out and constantly worried about it. Success does not mean selling out. Most actors are lucky to have been in constant work for over twenty years. He has a career and money in the bank and the offers are constantly coming in for work. He can now pick and choose pretty much anything that takes his fancy.

Martin is at a point in his life where he has never been happier. *Sherlock* is one of the biggest roles he will ever undertake and he receives more fan mail about the series than he does for *The Hobbit*, which says a great deal, considering the worldwide appeal and longevity of the Tolkien novel. *Sherlock* may even be the role Freeman is best membered for in years to come.

'I get more twelve-year-olds coming up to me than I used to,' he said to *The Independent*'s Emma Jones in 2013. 'But, I promise, I still have a lot of conversations with people that have no idea who I am. Which is great for me as I usually just want to eat a bowl of pasta in peace.'

Ten years later and people still ask Freeman about *The Office* and, though he is pleased to have moved on from being recognised as Tim Canterbury, he is delighted that the series is still highly thought of.

'I haven't seen Ricky Gervais for a while,' he said when asked by the *Daily Mirror*'s John Hiscock if he keeps in touch with his former *Office* colleagues. 'I saw Lucy Davis in a play and I see Mackenzie Crook once in a blue moon. We're moving on with our own lives, but I still have a tremendous affection for it.'

The Office was the role that broke his career and got the TV producers calling and the scripts rolling in. It is a show he is very proud of as both a viewer and an actor. There is enough distance now between Freeman and *The Office* for him not to get defensive about it anymore.

He remains uninterested in an *Office* reunion and, as with *Sherlock*, he believes that a short, sharp burst of creativity in just a few short years has greater impact than a long, drawn-out TV show that repeats and recycles its own ideas. The idea is to make the viewer crave more, not less. Freeman also prefers the idea of leaving something and moving on to the next project, as he gets rather restless and feels the urge to try his hand in different roles.

'Well, I think my general outlook on life is that things should be finite and things are finite,' Freeman told *TwoCentsTV*'s Anne Bayley. 'You know, we all die. Everything ends. And so for me the idea of things going on and on and on, I don't always find very attractive. But, you know, if it's a show that I love and it keeps going on and it retains its quality then I'm delighted to be a viewer of it.'

He said to *Nerd Repository*'s Kyle Wilson, 'I want to leave something, hopefully, leave something behind that people go, oh, that was great, as opposed to, oh, why did they carry on with this? It was good for the first three seasons and then it all went wrong. I'm well aware that some things don't go wrong after three seasons. Some of my favourite things are fantastic for a long time. But, yeah, for me personally, I like the hit-and-run approach. I love doing this for a bit and then doing something else for a bit and then doing something else for a bit. That's the way I'm hardwired I think.'

There's no question that people will ask him about *Sherlock* and *The Hobbit* in ten years' time and probably right up until his old age. But that's fine with him. There are many actors that would die to be given those chances in life. He does not take his success for granted and remains rather humble about it all. Having said that, he has put the hard graft in since his first on-screen role in *The Bill* all those years ago.

Although he made his career initially in TV, he does not see a difference between working in either TV or film. He is more interested in good writing than he is on the specific medium. He's attracted to strong roles more than anything else. Naturally, each role will be different but if the writing is of a high standard then he will be interested. Television will bring with it a different experience than film – there's usually more money floating around in film, better buffet lunches, nicer trailers and such – but the work in front of the camera is still the same. The things he's most proud of, such as *The Robinsons*, have not been seen widely.

Freeman continues to have a love-hate relationship with fame. It comes as part and parcel with the job. If he could get paid for buying records and clothes, he'd more than likely make a living out of it but acting is his profession and with it comes some pitfalls. It's not something he craves and nor is it something he can escape from. Not now. Not with *The Hobbit* and *Sherlock* being so successful on a global scale. *Fargo* was one of the most talked-about TV shows of 2014 and helped broaden Martin's name in the US but it also meant he had to cope with the level of fame it brought him. If he goes to the local coffee shop to buy a cup of coffee, he has to face the fact that there might be a photographer on his tail waiting to snap a shot of him to sell to a tabloid. If he's out shopping for records or clothes, he might – or rather, is more than likely to – get noticed by members of the public who'll approach him for an autograph or photo, or both.

He once said to *Empire* magazine, 'It's like when people say to me, "No really, it's a compliment, you're famous"; that's not a fucking compliment. Himmler was famous as well, you know what I mean? It's not a compliment.'

If he is with friends or family when someone approaches him for a photo or an autograph, he will politely decline, but he finds it's like he's taken food away from them. He has the right to say no but some fans don't see it that way; they see it almost as an obligation that Freeman has to always agree to a picture or autograph. Most of his fans do totally respect his privacy but social media has made it much harder to stay private. If Freeman commits to having a picture taken with a fan, it's going to be plastered all over the Internet on sites such as Twitter and Facebook. It's the shape of the modern world.

'If people ask to take pictures of me as me in the street, as they often do, then I say "Look, don't put it on Twitter, please" or I say "No thanks" or "Not when I'm with my family" or whatever I say,' he admitted to *Den of Geek*'s Louisa Mellor. 'I like the idea of not everything happening between two human beings to be *everyone's* property. Do you know what I mean? Because now, "Can I have a picture?" is the same as in my day, "Hello". So "Hello, nice to meet you" is now "Can I have a picture?" and then they get out the camera and people start to line up.'

Freeman is not as 'pathological' about his privacy as he once described. He's opened up in recent years, feeling more comfortable (but still guarded) about his partner and children as well as his background. He would give up a major Hollywood movie if it caused disruption to his family and home life. He is very family-orientated. Now that he is a household name and regularly seen on TV and in the cinema, he has learned that fame can be controlled. If some celebrity wants an entourage following them around with great fanfare, they have no cause to complain about the publicity and hounding from the paparazzi they might get. Freeman is less interested in causing a publicity stir.

Does he want his own children to get into acting?

'I wouldn't actively encourage or discourage them from this life,' he once said to *Future Movies*' Paul Gallagher. 'Both me and my other half are actors and, while of course there are hard bits to it, it's a good life and I'm thankful to it every day. But I think if you're the children of actors you don't need encouragement – you've got a bit of it in you. So I'm just gonna see where that goes with mine.'

Freeman spoke to *TV Choice* magazine's Martina Fowler about life as a dad and its rewards: 'Just all the positive stuff that it gives you, and the way that you improve as a human being, in that you become better by helping someone else be better. The downside of it is you suddenly realise how selfish you are, or how selfish you're allowed to be in your life up to the point of being a parent. I thought I was a nice person before I became a dad and then I thought, "Christ, I'm not, I'm selfish, self-obsessed, and impatient." I think until you've been a parent nothing else has tested you like that. No one winds you up the way a baby will!'

As a dad, he has said in interviews that he doesn't want his kids to see him as anything but their dad, so that means they haven't seen his films or TV shows. Maybe his children don't have any idea just how famous their dad is?

'I want to keep my children absolutely out of it until they're of an age where they can decide,' he admitted to the *New Zealand Herald*. 'Sometimes when I'm stopped in the street and I'm with my children, I always try and get them out of the picture and they'll go, "Why don't you want us?" and I'm like, "No, I'm protecting you!"'

Wind-down time for Freeman is relaxing with his partner at home watching a DVD box-set such as the Kevin Spacey-led political drama *House of Cards*, or having a day out with the family or a trip to his local record stores to uncover some vinyl gems for his ever-growing collection. He has a terrific relationship with his partner – there is humour, trust, loyalty, love.

As an avid music fan and vinyl junkie, it would be interesting to see Freeman cast in a music biopic. Although whether he would commit to such a project is a different matter. He's always said he's glad he was not a fan of *The Hobbit* growing up because it would have changed his approach to the role, so perhaps playing Paul Weller or Paul McCartney in a film would have an impact on his performance. Given his age, he would perhaps be better suited as Beatles' producer George Martin or former Rolling Stones manager Andrew Loog Oldham. His fellow *Hobbit* star Andy Serkis once played Ian Dury in *Sex & Drugs & Rock & Roll*. Freeman is a fan of such music-based films as *24 Hour Party People*, which he rates very highly so, if a project of a similar nature should come across his desk, there's a chance he'd sign on the dotted line.

As 2015 approached, Martin Freeman had become one of the most respected and famous British actors working in film and TV. He stays close to his British roots and has not deserted his background in TV on this small island, though he is becoming increasingly popular in the USA. Where his career will go to next is anyone's guess but he is likely to continue to surprise and astound us with a wide range of memorable performances.

'He will only do things that he thinks are great,' commented *Sherlock* co-creator Steven Moffat to *The Guardian*'s John Plunkett. 'He is incredibly serious about acting, concentrating fiercely to the point where he can give himself a bad day. He can be a borderline grump if he feels he is having trouble, grumpy in the way that someone doing difficult sums is grumpy.'

Given his recent roles as Lester Nygaard and Richard III, one wonders if Freeman will shed his nice-guy image once and for all.

'I don't get cast as the guy who steps off a yacht in a white linen suit with a martini,' he once told *Entertainment Weekly*'s Josh

Rottenberg. 'It would not really be my function to be the smooth guy – unless something shitty happens to the smooth guy.'

There is a degree of uncertainty about acting and the entertainment-and-arts industry that allures Freeman.

'I like uncertainty in roles, and I like uncertainty in art, really,' Martin said to *Stuff.co.nz*'s Tom Cardy. 'And in theatrical terms, I'm not a massive fan of certainty. Without sounding overly pompous about it, I don't really trust certainty in anything, actually. Especially as I get older. Except love, I'm certain of love, I guess. But beliefs, characteristics, all that, I think everything is uncertain. And so I like playing people who reflect that, 'cause I think it's honest. I don't really believe it if it's certain, you know what I mean? I just don't buy it.'

It is more than likely that one day Freeman will be spoken about in the same breath as such revered actors of the stage and screen as Alec Guinness, Anthony Hopkins and Peter Cushing.

His star continues to shine.

SELECTIVE CREDITS

What follows is a list of Martin Freeman's roles in all mediums.

FILM

The Low Down (2000)

Ali G Indahouse (2002)

Love Actually (2003)

Shaun of the Dead (2004)

The Hitchhiker's Guide to the Galaxy (2005)

Confetti (2006)

Breaking and Entering (2006)

Long Hot Summer (2006)

Dedication (2007)

The Good Night (2007)

Hot Fuzz (2007)

The All Together (2007)

Nightwatching (2007)

Nativity! (2009)

Wild Target (2010)

Swinging with the Finkels (2011)

What's Your Number? (2011)

The Pirates! In an Adventure with Scientists! (aka *The Pirates! Band of Misfits*) (2012)

Animals (2012)

The Hobbit: An Unexpected Journey (2012)

Svengali (2013)

The World's End (2013)

Saving Santa (2013)

The Hobbit: The Desolation of Smaug (2013)

The Hobbit: The Battle of the Five Armies (2014)

TV SERIES

The Bill ('Mantrap', 1997)

This Life ('Last Tango In Southwark', 1997)

Casualty ('She Loved The Rain', 1998)

Picking Up The Pieces (Episode 1.7, 1998)

Exhaust (1999)

Bruiser (2000)

Lock, Stock... (2000)

Black Books ('Cooking The Books', 2000)

World of Pub (2001)

The Office (2001–2003)

Helen West (2002)

Linda Green ('Easy Come, Easy Go', 2002)

Charles II: The Power and The Passion (2003)

Hardware (2003–2004)
The Robinsons (2005)
Comedy Showcase ('Other People', 2007)
When Were We Funniest? (2008)
Boy Meets Girl (2009)
Sherlock (2010–2014)
Fargo (2014)

TV MOVIES
Men Only (2001)
Comic Relief: The Big Hair Do (2003)
The Debt (2003)
Margery and Gladys (2003)
Pride (2004)
Not Tonight with John Sergeant (2005)
The Old Curiosity Shop (2007)
Svengali (2009)
Micro Men (2009)
The Eichmann Show (2015)

SHORT FILMS
I Just Want to Kiss You (1998)
Fancy Dress (2001)
Call Register (2004)
Round About Five (2005)
Blake's Junction 7 (2005)
Lonely Hearts (2007)
Rubbish (2007)
HIV: The Musical (2009)

The Girl Is Mime (2010)
So You Want To Be A Pirate! (2012)
The Voorman Problem (2012)

STAGE

La Dispute (1999)
Jump Mr Malinoff, Jump (2000)
Kosher Harry (2002)
Blue Eyes and Heels (2005)
The Exonerated (2006)
The Last Laugh (2007)
Clybourne Park (2010)
Richard III (2014)

RADIO

The Great Unknown (BBC Radio 2, 2006)
The Steve Show (BBC 6Music, 2008)
The Unfortunates (BBC Radio 3, 2010)
Soul Show's New Year's Day Special (BBC Radio 2, 2014)

DOCUMENTARY

Rembrandt's J'Accuse (2008)

VIDEO GAMES

LEGO The Hobbit: The Video Game (2014)

MUSIC

Martin Freeman Presents... Made To Measure (2006)

SOURCES

The following print and online media was invaluable during the researching and writing of this biography. Thank you to every publication.

PRINT

Chicago Sun-Times

Daily Mirror

Daily Telegraph

Financial Times

The Globe and Mail

The Independent

Mail On Sunday

Metro

The Observer

The Sunday Times

The Times

Time Out

The Washington Post

ONLINE

http://www.aintitcool.com

http://britishtheatreguide.info

http://collider.com

http://dorkshelf.com

http://exclaim.ca

http://articles.latimes.com

http://londoncalling.com

http://movies.about.com

http://nerdrepository.com

http://news.asiaone.com

http://news.bbc.co.uk

http://nycmovieguru.com

http://twocentstv.com

http://uk.askmen.com

http://uk.ign.com

http://variety.com

www.3news.co.nz

www.avclub.com

www.bbc.co.uk

www.beyondthejoke.co.uk

www.cinemablend.com

www.comedy.co.uk

www.contactmusic.com

www.dailymail.co.uk

www.darkhorizons.com

www.denofgeek.com

www.digitalspy.co.uk

www.dvdtalk.com

www.dvdverdict.com

www.empireonline.com

www.esquire.co.uk

www.ew.com

www.express.co.uk

www.flicksandbits.com

www.futuremovies.co.uk

www.gq-magazine.co.uk

www.theguardian.com

www.hampshire-life.co.uk

www.hitfix.com

www.hollywood.com

www.hollywoodreporter.com

www.indielondon.co.uk

www.indiewire.com

www.inspiremagazine.org.uk

www.lastbroadcast.co.uk

www.latino-review.com

www.mediamikes.com

www.mirror.co.uk

www.movieweb.com

www.musicomh.com

www.nerve.com

www.nydailynews.com

www.nytimes.com

www.nzherald.co.nz

www.radiotimes.com

www.readersdigest.co.nz

SOURCES

www.rte.ie

www.scotsman.com

www.sfgate.com

www.shortlist.com

www.smh.com.au

www.splicedwire.com

www.stagenoise.com

www.standard.co.uk

www.stuff.co.nz

www.telegraph.co.uk

www.timeout.com

www.tinymixtapes.com

www.totalfilm.com

www.tvchoicemagazine.co.uk

www.tvguide.co.uk

www.universityobserver.ie

www.usatoday.com

www.vulture.com

www.walesonline.co.uk

www.washingtonpost.com

ACKNOWLEDGEMENTS

Thank you to the following writers, journalists and authors whose work was integral in researching and writing this biography:

Carlos Aguilar, Ethan Alter, Andrew Anthony, Michael Arbeiter, Nick Aveling, Steven Balbirnie, Anne Bayley, Gabby Bermingham, Robert Bianco, Michael Billington, Aaron Birch, Rob Blackwelder, Rob Bleaney, Peter Bradshaw, Ben Brantley, Simon Brew, Georgina Brown, Christopher Campbell, Capone, Tom Cardy, Rob Carnevale, Jeannette Catsoulis, Dominic Cavendish, Paul Connolly, Rachel Cooke, Richard Corliss, Maddy Costa, Simon Crook, Manohla Dargis, Michael Deacon, Bruce Dessau, Amanda DeWees, Emma Didbin, Claire Dikecoglu, Andrew Duncan, Tom Eames, Angie Errigo, Euan Ferguson, Daniel Fienberg, Paul Fischer, Kathryn Flett, Jack

Foley, Tyler Foster, Martina Fowler, Garth Franklin, Oliver Franklin, Philip French, Philo Gabriel, Paul Gallagher, Mark Gatiss, Mike Gencarelli, Olly Grant, Frank Grice, Mike Hale, Robert Hanks, Kevin Harley, Jesse Hassenger, Sarah Hemming, David Hinkley, John Hiscock, Henry Hitchings, Michael Hogan, Michael Holden, Jonathan Holland, Travis Mackenzie Hoover, Simon Houpt, Tim Huddleston, David Jenkins, Ellen E. Jones, Emma Jones, Morgan Jeffery, Dan Jolin, Ellen E Jones, Danuta Kean, Rhoda Koenig, Tom Lamont, Peter Lathan, Ben Lawrence, Susanna Lazarus, Alana Lee, Matthew Leyland, Brian Lowery, Denise Martin, Matt Maytum, Gareth McLean, Caroline McGinn, Craig McLean, Louisa Mellor, Stephanie Merritt, Tom Morgan, Rebecca Murray, Hannah Nathanson, Kim Newman, Philiana Ng, Hanh Nguyen, Phelim O'Neill, Robin Oliver, Ken P., Andrew Parker, Anthony Pearce, Cindy Pearlman, John Plunkett, Vicki Power, John Preston, Tony Purnell, Libby Purves, Anthony Quinn, Nathan Rabin, Christina Radish, James Rampton, Katey Rich, Olly Richards, Tim Robey, James Rocchi, Kate Rodger, Julian Roman, Jonathan Romney, Josh Rottenberg, Sukhdev Sandhu, Lisa Schwarzbaum, A.O. Scott, Nick de Semlyen, David Sexton, Jane Simon, Leigh Singer, Adam Smith, Nancy Banks-Smith, Neil Smith, Rupert Smith, Jason Solomons, Charles Spencer, Cheryl Stonehouse, Hank Stuever, Chris Sullivan, Siobhan Synnot, John Thaxter, Paul Taylor, Michael Thomson, Alexis Tirado, Gabe Toro, Kenneth Turan, Karen Valby, Alona Wartofsky, Darren Waters, Jamie Watt, Steve 'Frosty' Weintraub, Jay Weissberg, David Wiegand, Alice Wignall, Andrew Williams, Benji Wilson, Kyle Wilson, Neil Young and Jordan Zakarin.

ACKNOWLEDGEMENTS

Thank you also to Chris Mitchell and the staff at John Blake Publishing.

Apologies if I have missed out any names; it was not intentional.

Visit the author's website at www.neildanielsbooks.com